THE WORKS IN ARCHITECTURE OF ROBERT AND JAMES ADAM

Portrait of Robert Adam *attributed to Johann Zoffany* (*1734/5–1810*) *Oil on canvas. 50 x 40 ins.*
National Portrait Gallery, London.

THE WORKS IN ARCHITECTURE OF ROBERT AND JAMES ADAM

EDITED WITH
AN INTRODUCTION BY
ROBERT ORESKO

ACADEMY EDITIONS · LONDON
ST. MARTIN'S PRESS · NEW YORK

FOR J. PETER KING

Published in Great Britain in 1975 by
Academy Editions 7 Holland Street London W8
SBN 85670 034 7

Published in the U.S.A. in 1975 by St. Martin's Press Inc.
175 Fifth Avenue New York N.Y. 10010
Library of Congress Catalog Card Number 74-78170
Text set in 12/15 pt. Monotype Caslon, printed by photolithography, and
bound in Great Britain at The Pitman Press, Bath

CONTENTS

ACKNOWLEDGMENTS

The following must be acknowledged for their kind assistance: Dr George Zarnecki of the Courtauld Institute of Art, London, for his aid in obtaining a fine series of photographs of Syon House (pp. 12, 13), of Shelburne House (p. 34) and of the Williams Wynn House (pp. 9, 27, 29, 30, 31, 34); Mr G. L. Conran for photographs of Kenwood House (pp. 18, 20, 21, 22); *The Weekly Scotsman* for the photographs of the University of Edinburgh (pp. 41, 42); Mr Cecil Farthing for his help with photographs from the National Buildings Record (pp. 33, 34); the Royal Society of Arts for the photograph of their building (p. 23); the Distillers Company Ltd. for permission to photograph the Williams Wynn House; and the Wernher Collection for the photograph of Luton Park House (p. 14). The National Portrait Gallery, London, kindly granted permission for the reproduction of their portrait of Robert Adam, and the Courtauld Institute of Art, London, most graciously lent the Thézard version of *The Works*, used as the basis of the current edition. Mention must also be made of the contribution of the late John Swarbrick, whose earlier version of *The Works* helped to pave the way for this volume.

It gives me the greatest pleasure to thank Mr Kenneth King, Miss Jill A. Kraye, Mrs Gordon McDermid, Mr Richard Maelzer and Mr Harold Rubin, all of whom read the manuscript and offered useful suggestions, and Helen Lady Dashwood and Mr David Peet, whose advice saved me from making many errors. A massive debt of gratitude is due to Miss Shelagh Johnson, whose assistance on the research and planning of this volume was invaluable.

FOREWORD

The Works in Architecture of Robert and James Adam was published in three volumes over a period of fifty years. The first volume, which contains the most extensive and detailed discussion of Adam's artistic credo, consists of five parts and appeared first as consecutive instalments in 1773, 1774, 1775, 1776 and 1778. These were issued as a single volume in 1778. Volume two, which was also published first in five instalments, was brought out in 1779, with a very rare second edition following in 1786. The third volume, with the barest commentary, appeared in 1822, nearly thirty years after the deaths of Robert and James Adam.

Selections from the plates which Adam commissioned for *The Works* have been used frequently by biographers and architectural historians throughout the nineteenth and twentieth centuries to illustrate the decorative style evolved by the brothers. In 1931 John Tiranti published the complete corpus of engravings and Adam's preface to the 1778 edition but excluded the remainder of the text. The prefaces and explanations of the plates were totally absent from Alec Tiranti's 1959 reprint of *The Works*, although this edition did include a biographical essay by John Swarbrick.

This new edition of *The Works* brings the complete text and all the engravings together in a single volume and is based upon the reprint of E. Thézard Fils (Dourdan, France, 1902), which utilised the first complete editions of each volume. The present edition, however, differs from Thézard's in several respects. First of all, the prefaces to the volumes and the explanations of all the plates have been combined into a single section of text, maintaining the sequence of the original publication. The first edition of *The Works* was bilingual, with one column in English matched on each page by a French translation, a procedure which betrayed both Adam's concern for his clients in France and his desire to increase his prestige on the continent. The current edition eliminates the French translation. In addition, the plates have been reassembled entirely so that all of Adam's designs for a specific building are grouped together, regardless of the volume in which they appeared first. This alteration has been undertaken to ensure a unified visual appreciation of the full range of Adam's work for each separate commission. Nevertheless, the original position of every engraving in the three volumes has been specified on the pages which introduce each section of plates, and these numbers correspond to the location of Adam's descriptions in his text. Besides an entirely new introductory essay, this edition also includes an up-to-date bibliography, indexes of buildings and engravers and over forty-five photographs documenting the achievement of the firm of Adam Bros.

1. The Williams Wynn House. A detail from the chimney piece from the music room.

ROBERT ADAM

Following Robert Adam's death on 3 March 1792, the *Gentleman's Magazine* printed an obituary lamenting the passing of one of Britain's great architects and designers. "Mr Adam," it concluded, "produced a total change in the architecture of this country." Robert Adam would have agreed. In the preface to the first volume of *The Works in Architecture of Robert and James Adam* the brothers announced with characteristic firmness and self-assurance that their designs had "brought about, in this country, a kind of revolution in the whole system of this useful and elegant art." Art historians have questioned the originality of the Adam innovations and have modified their view of the speed with which they were adopted, but it is still undeniable that English architecture and especially English interior design were radically different after Robert Adam's three decades in London.

While the arts in France, Italy, Bavaria and Austria were dominated by the florid patterns and curved forms of the Rococo, Britain, in the first half of the eighteenth century, remained on the steady course charted by Lord Burlington, William Kent and other members of the solid English Palladian school. These architects and theorists looked upon Inigo Jones, Andrea Palladio and beyond them to Vitruvius as their household deities; the writings and works of these three masters constituted for the Burlingtonians an architectural canon, inviolable in both its precise, albeit limited, vocabulary of detail and the methods by which these specific parts could be arranged and combined into a single, whole unit. Certainly Robert Adam saw his own work, at least in part, as an attack upon what was by 1760 the architectural *ancien régime*. He disparaged Jones and Palladio in letters dated as early as 1756, and his brother and future colleague, James Adam, after visiting Vicenza, recorded his disappointment with Palladio's designs, which he found "ill-adjusted both in their plans and elevations."

Robert Adam objected to the unrelenting and dreary heaviness, what he saw as the inherent stodginess, of the strictly controlled Palladian forms. These characteristics were most clearly represented in his mind by the massive and deeply carved entablatures and pediments of façade design and by the rigidly compartmented ceilings, dominating marble fireplaces, vigorous stucco work and elaborate door frames, often crowned by a broken pediment, which were so prevalent in Palladian interior decoration. But Adam's critical reaction to Palladianism extended beyond his dislike of its specific stylistic components and developed into an attack upon the Palladian method of artistic expression. According to Adam, the architectural schools of the Renaissance, Mannerist and Baroque periods had fossilised the rules and standards implicit in the masterpieces of classical

2. *Syon House. The chimney piece wall from the ante-room.*

3. Syon House. The library or gallery.

4. Syon House. The end wall from the library or gallery.

5. Syon House. A detail from the library or gallery with the portrait of Hugh Smithson, first duke of Northumberland.

Greece and Rome. These theorists, by codifying the artistic laws of the ancients, had removed the sense of freedom and liberty of expression which, in Adam's view, were essential to the creative process. In turn, this rigidity had resulted in the perpetuation of designs which were at once uninspired and monotonously heavy. "The great masters of antiquity," he wrote, "were not so rigidly scrupulous, they varied the proportions as the general spirit of their composition required, clearly perceiving that, however necessary these rules may be to form the taste and to arrest the licentiousness of the scholar, they often cramp the genius, and circumscribe the ideas of the master."

It must always be remembered that despite these frontal assaults upon his immediate architectural predecessors, Robert Adam drew, sometimes directly, upon the experience of the very men he attacked. Yet it is equally certain that both Adam and his contemporaries saw his new style as something quite distinct from what had gone before. The Adam style, as it developed in the early 1760's, constituted a return to the purity of the artistic expression of the classical, pre-Christian world. On one level this meant the archaeological exploration followed by the utilisation of an extended vocabulary of antique forms, while, on a more basic and less easily definable plane, it necessitated the revival of the classical spirit for the use of these rediscovered elements. The Renaissance had deformed the past by its rigid adherence to and widespread application of certain specific, sometimes isolated, examples and, according to Adam, had thus missed the essential lesson of the antique. This dogmatism had to be removed and replaced by the less restricted although authentically classical conception of a varying manipulation of forms for each specific and different occasion. The ancients taught that elements could not be combined and applied in exactly the same way for every occasion, but had to change in order to meet the peculiar needs of a specific time and place. The scheme of a Roman temple, for instance, should not be blindly applied to a private home, but the determination of which general mode and which specific details fit a particular situation had to be left to the discretion and genius of the individual artist not to the dictates of a long-dead theorist. This resolve both to expand the eighteenth century's knowledge of the antique and to renew its liberating methods of creativity placed Robert Adam firmly in the rich tradition of the Neo-Classical movement. The irony exists in that while Adam, in the name of a return to an unsullied view of the past, led English design from the heaviness of Palladianism to his own lighter, more elegant, almost effeminate mode,

6. Syon House. The entrance gateway and screen.

7. Syon House. A detail from the ante-room with the trophies adapted from those of Octavianus Augustus.

8. Syon House. The chimney piece from the red drawing room.

9. The Parish Church, Mistley. The twin towers, after the demolition of the main body of the church.

10. Luton Park House. The east front, with the alterations of 1816 and 1903.

11. Kedleston. The central feature from the south front.

the French Neo-Classicists, fired by principles identical to Adam's, reacted against the Rococo in favour of the more solid, assertively masculine *goût grec*.

But despite this divergence from the attitudes of continental Neo-Classicism, Adam yielded place to none in his enthusiasm for the antique. Perhaps the most important episodes in the development of Adam's consciousness of the classical world occurred during the years (1754–1758) spent on the Grand Tour. Keenly ambitious in whatever engaged his efforts, he was determined to make a major contribution to his century's rapidly expanding awareness of antiquity. This ultimately took the form of an expedition to survey the remains of Diocletian's palace at Spalato (the modern Split). The impressive folio, *Ruins of the Palace of the Emperor Diocletian at Spalatro in Dalmatia*, was published in 1764. It immediately elevated Adam's position as an antiquarian to one alongside those of Robert Wood, James Stuart and Nicholas Revett, whose volumes describing their investigations at Palmyra, Baalbec and Athens set the standards for architectural scholarship in the eighteenth century. But Adam's ex-

12. Syon House. The hall with the ascent to the ante-room.

13. Osterley Park. The Etruscan room.

plorations during his Grand Tour did not aim solely at establishing his name as a connoisseur. As with Inigo Jones during his journeys to the continent, Robert Adam systematically constructed what in modern jargon might be called a vastly expanded data bank of classical architectural designs and motifs. In letters to his family, he explained his habit of collecting "antique cornices, friezes, figures, bas reliefs, vases, altars" and of "employing painters, drawers, etc. to do the fountains, the buildings, the statues and the things that are of use for drawing after and for giving hints to the imagination of us modern devils." James Adam proceeded in an identical manner during his Grand Tour (1760–1763), and his diaries are crammed with references to sketches of paintings, fountains and ruins either made by the younger Adam himself or commissioned by him from other artists. As Sir John Summerson pointed out, one of the main purposes of Adam's studies in Italy was to make him "the unquestioned master and supreme authority" of antique

14. The Williams Wynn House. The staircase.

15. The Admiralty screen, Whitehall.

16. Kenwood House. A mirror from the library.

design. These sketches and relics brought back to England constituted at once the concrete record of the sites and antiquities which Robert and James Adam hunted out and also a vitally important source book for future commissions. The imagination of both brothers fed upon the antique, and many elements in their later designs can be traced directly to these drawings made during the years both were on the continent.

Crucial as this first-hand, on-the-spot research and recording were to Robert Adam's artistic vision and to his architectural vocabulary, the Grand Tour explorations did not constitute the only source for his knowledge of the antique. Obviously, the published findings of earlier investigators, both English and French, broadened his view of the classical epoch. Robert Wood's *Ruins of Palmyra* (1753) was especially influential in this respect, perhaps even more so than Adam's own examination of Diocletian's palace. Adam's five weeks in Dalmatia, while resulting in an important piece of scholarship, left few contributions to his own decorative style. Only the specially devised composite order, consisting of a single row of acanthus leaves beneath fluting, can be traced to the inspiration of Spalato, whereas Wood's engravings of the Palmyran ruins, never visited by Adam, provided the schemes for several well-known Adam ceilings, most importantly one at Osterley.

The classical world was quite clearly the strongest single inspiration for Robert Adam's genius. The influence of the antique is apparent in every Adam room from the most precise details and fixtures to the undefinable ambiance and general spirit. A few examples, repre-

17. Kenwood House. The library.

18. Kenwood House. The north front.

19. Kenwood House. The south or park front.

sentative of his entire *œuvre*, must suffice. A frieze from the Forum of Trajan was included in the gallery of Croome Court, the trophies of Octavianus Augustus were adapted for the Syon House ante-room decoration, while, on a slightly larger scale, a carpet designed for the gallery at Syon was probably derived from an Ostia mosaic. Innumerable ceiling patterns were antique transplants, the unexecuted sketch for one at Audley End, for example, coming from the Baths of Augustus, while volutes, mouldings and orders all had specific classical prototypes. Adam's fondness for the combination of columnar screen and apse was similarly derived from the antique basilica pattern, while his barrel vaulted ceilings had an equally impeccable classical pedigree. But perhaps the importance of the ancient world for Adam's vision was most firmly and unequivocably asserted in the south façade of Kedleston, into which was imbedded a model of the Arch of Constantine.

It should be obvious, even from this highly selective list of classical borrowings, that Adam's antique inspiration was largely Roman, not Greek. In the controversy which raged among Neo-Classicists as to the predominance of either Hellenistic or Roman culture, Adam conceded that Greece was the fountainhead of the true and pure art. For instance, in the frontispiece to *The*

20. Kenwood House. A detail from the half dome of the library.

Works, engraved by Bartolozzi after a design by Antonio Zucchi, Greece appears on a map below Italy in order to signify her position as the root, the source of the Roman achievement. Yet in the practical application of his decorative schemes, Greek motifs played a very small role. The major influence was Roman. Indeed, one of Adam's most striking contributions to concepts of design dealt with Roman domestic interiors, which he rightly pointed out were totally different from and much more restrained than the grandiose temple schemes thoughtlessly applied by Baroque architects to the interiors of private homes.

But if the classical strain was by far the most pronounced in Adam's schemes, it was not the only outside influence. Although the intensity and sincerity of his disapproval of various aspects of Renaissance and Baroque style must never be discounted, these periods left many telling and unmistakeable marks upon Adam's own designs. The most obvious legacy from the *cinquecento* were the flat panels of *grottesche*, elaborately decorative and convoluted arabesque, which Adam derived principally from the designs of Raphael, Giulio Romano and Giovanni da Udine. Although Adam's *grottesche* may have lacked the vigour of those in the Vatican *loggie* or the Villa Madama, the debt to the high Renaissance is clear. Similarly, the elaborate stucco work at the Villa Pamphili, executed largely under the direction of Alessandro Algardi in 1644–1652, also contributed to the development of the Adam style. Indeed, in many ways Adam envied the Renaissance, which, he felt, was closer in time to the antique world and which had the benefit of living with classical ruins and interior designs which had disappeared by the middle of the eighteenth century. "In the times of Raphael, Polidoro, Giovanni da Udine, Vasari, Zuchero and Algardi," the brothers noted, "there is no doubt that there were much greater remains of the grotte, than what are now to be seen." Examples of his borrowings from this period can be multiplied easily; the Pulteney Bridge in Bath (1770), for instance, was modelled upon the pattern of the Ponte Vecchio in Florence. Even the much castigated Palladio was not without his effect, and Adam continued to use selected Palladian elements. The triple compartmented window, set into relieving arches, most clearly betrays the influence of the Venetian master.

The work of Adam's immediate English predecessors, however stodgy and tradition-bound it may have seemed to him, nevertheless, was important for the formation of his style. Burlingtonian prototypes for chimney pieces, adorned with terms and caryatids and with console supported mantel shelves, were the immediate progenitors for Adam's own conception of this important decorative feature, and he remained firmly convinced by the concept of "movement," derived from the Renaissance Italian theorists but also used by such English Palladians as Kent and such non-Palladians as Vanbrugh. In a famous and much-quoted explanation, Robert Adam defined "movement" as "the rise and fall, the advance and recess, with other diversity of form, in the different parts of a building, so as to add greatly to the picturesque of the composition." In his façade design this meant not only the breaking forward of various elements, a typically Baroque technique, but also the strongly defined outline of buildings as demonstrated by the fractured silhouette and "staccato" disposition inherent in Kent's and Burlington's Palladianism. This architectural quality of "movement" is less apparent in Adam's interior designs (although even here the effects of vaults and apses seem related to this concept), and "movement" found instead a different expression in the elegant and pictorial surface decoration for the insides of houses. His lack of enthusiasm for the plain, unadorned surface may, in fact, have been a major artistic inheritance from his father, William Adam, the leading Scottish Palladian architect of his day.

But if Robert Adam benefited from the experience of

these varied predecessors, he also learned from his contemporaries. The question of French influence is a difficult one and provides, perhaps, a classic case of mutual artistic pollination. Certainly many French designers aped the Adam style from the late 1760's onwards, an important manifestation of the Anglomania in vogue during the French Enlightenment. But it seems more than probable that Adam, especially in his furniture design during his early years, experimented with French modes. The projects of Soufflot for Gobelins interior decoration possibly could have provided the direct inspiration for Adam's window stool at Croome Court, and in the middle 1760's he may have worked with some of Poirier's designs. As Eileen Harris pointed out, Neufforge's *Recueil d'Architecture* seemed to hold great interest for Adam, and the use of medallions to cover furniture surfaces and the linking of a tall mirror to a table in order to form an entire wall decoration, two favourite Adam techniques, may well have come originally from this source.

Adam, still an impressionable young man while on the Grand Tour, was also deeply influenced by Giovanni Battista Piranesi. Although its roots were firmly planted during the years Adam was abroad, the friendship with Piranesi did not end with the Scot's return home in 1758. Piranesi dedicated his *Campus Martius* (1762) to "Roberto Adam Britann. Architecto Celebirrim," and the Italian also engraved four plates for *The Works*. Piranesi's influence seems to have been very great while they were together in Italy and continued when they were separated, through the medium of his theoretical writings. The Italian's knowledge of and enthusiam for archaeological remains provided a common bond of interest. Adam's taste for the grand may have been another gift of this friendship, and some of Adam's chimney piece designs and perhaps even elements of the famous Etruscan mode of room decoration seem to have been derived from Piranesi's *Diverse maniere* of 1769.

But probably the most important and wide-reaching effect Piranesi had upon his friend was the transmission of his notion of artistic licence. The concept of abstracting the elements of classical culture and then rearranging them into a pattern of one's own was developed and expounded largely by Piranesi. As with Inigo Jones, it is obvious that Robert Adam cast his intellectual net widely and borrowed from a staggeringly rich variety of classical, Renaissance, Baroque and contemporary sources. But, as again with Jones, this scholarly tabulation of a seemingly inexhaustible number of architectural details and the concomitant reliance upon earlier modes for inspiration did not result in Adam's being a mere copyist or *pasticheur*. Elaborating upon Piranesi's doctrine of artistic licence and relying upon what he saw as the authentically classical approval of the individual artist's unique genius, Adam blended his elements, whatever their source, into his own personal manner, and the compound which resulted was always pure Adam.

21. Kenwood House. A detail from the south or park front.

As we have seen already, Robert Adam was convinced that this combination and re-combination of specific elements to fit specific situations was the precise method used by the great masters of antiquity before their motifs were formalised into an unnatural and ostensibly inviolable régime by the Renaissance theorists. In a famous letter to Lord Kames, Adam discussed his use of the doric order and mentioned that "I have ventured to alter some parts of this order, particularly in its mouldings; rejecting some of the common ones, and adopting and substituting others in their stead." We have an excellent example of Adam's flexibility with orders in his adaptation of an ionic capital to the anteroom at Syon House. The volutes and the mouldings were borrowed from the ionic order of the Erechtheum as illustrated in Le Roy's *Les ruines des plus beaux monuments de la Grèce*. But rather than use the necking of Le Roy's ionic order for the Syon capital, Adam turned instead to a type found in Roman *thermae*. Le Roy's design for the ionic necking was not discarded, however, but instead of appearing in the Syon capital, it was used as decoration for the frieze of the entablature in the same room. This specific case is typical of the free wheeling compositional malleability which was, perhaps, the quintessential feature of the Adam style. Only rarely were his prototypes, classical or Renaissance, mechanically reproduced without alteration, and there

22. Kenwood House. The half dome and a detail from the corinthian screen of the library.

23. The Society of Arts. The street front.

were innumerable cases of elements, which, while obviously derived from a specific source, nevertheless bore equally clearly the Adam imprint. Adam's *grottesche* were closely related to those of Raphael and his followers, yet the light, linear, flat elegance of Adam's made them quite distinct from the vigorous, exuberant contortions in the Vatican. The frieze in the gallery at Croome Court, while derived from the Forum of Trajan, is also an altered form of its ancestor, more subdued, flattened and restored; while in the process of transfer to Osterley the ceiling of the Temple of the Sun at Palmyra lost its square and circle and acquired instead rectangular and oval borders with over-sized feathers. Clearly, Adam experimented with his designs, changing individual components with freedom and ease and combining elements in ways which were entirely original but which conformed to the standards of his own impeccable taste. Adam sounded a note of caution in his letter to Lord Kames, warning that this flexible procedure was not without danger and "may do harm in the hands of rash innovators or mere retailers in the art, who have neither eyes nor judgment." Needless to say, these strictures did not apply to Robert Adam himself,

24. The Adelphi. A view of the river front from a print (1796) by Thomas Malton.

and his style remained, to use Sir John Summerson's typically lucid summation, "a personal revision and reconstitution of the antique into which many threads from a variety of sources were drawn and interwoven."

It was the graceful achievement of a unified whole through the blending of divergent elements which was Adam's primary contribution to the development of design. The rooms which he decorated were carefully orchestrated in terms of ornament, colour and furniture. The painstaking attention to detail is apparent in all of his work. Large patches of white were avoided because Adam found them too glaring when compared to his gentle and muted blues and greens or to the more striking Etruscan combination of ochre, black and cream. Similarly, Adam paid close attention to the furnishings of the rooms he designed and decorated. Although the number of houses for which he provided the entire range of furniture is very small, Adam was at times consulted on the fitting-out of his rooms and more than occasionally designed those pieces, such as tall mirrors and tables, which formed a composition and were considered to be wall decoration, thus removed

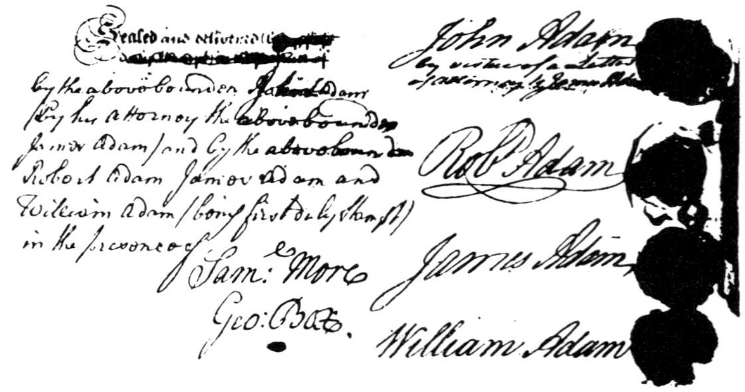

25. The signatures of the four Adam brothers.

from the province of the cabinet maker. It was this control over as many aspects as possible of the decoration that gave an Adam room its unique sense of completeness and total conception, an achievement which resulted in Adam's reputation being more solidly grounded upon his interior designs for buildings than upon his exterior schemes. Adam was only rarely asked by a client to plan a building from the ground up. Most often, as at Kedleston, he took over the construction of the house from another architect, or, as at Syon, he was

26. The Adelphi. A view of the Royal Terrace from a print (1795) by Thomas Malton.

27. Osterley Park. The double portico entrance to the inner courtyard.

commissioned to transform only the interiors of an existing building. Adam increasingly came to be viewed as an artist uniquely equipped to solve specific difficulties, one who could construct a consistently elegant, Neo-Classical interior in Jacobean shaped rooms and could make the box-like limits of London town houses seem spacious and graceful. His most notable achievements are embodied in his interior designs.

This concentration on interiors must have come as a deep disappointment to Adam, who longed to plan and construct from the beginning a giant, public commission for the capital. The great opportunity, such as that given to his rival, Sir William Chambers, at Somerset House, eluded him. Several reasons have been put forward to explain this neglect, including the supposed antipathy of George III and the all too real opposition of the powerful Chambers, who, good Burlingtonian that he was, disliked what he considered to be Adam's frivolity. For whatever causes, Adam felt blocked in his desire to plan on a grand scale and turned, perhaps in part as compensation, to a series of privately financed, almost town planning ventures. The Adelphi project and his unexecuted designs for a series of mansions in Portland Place and for the development of Bath all fall into this category. Only during the last decade of his life, when his activities centred increasingly upon the re-building of Edinburgh, did Adam seem to have his great undertaking within his grasp.

The Scottish commissions of his last years represented, in some ways, a homecoming for Robert Adam.

28. The Williams Wynn House. A detail from the ceiling of the second withdrawing room.

Born in Kirkcaldy on 3 July 1728, Robert Adam belonged to a family which numbered among its friends many of the luminaries of the Scottish Enlightenment. Adam Smith, David Hume, Adam Ferguson and Alexander Carlyle were all frequent visitors to the Adam house. Moreover, the Adam family itself made distinguished contributions to the intellectual and artistic achievement of the north. William Robertson, one of the outstanding historians of the eighteenth century, was Robert Adam's cousin, and William Adam, the patriarch of the clan, was the most eminent Scottish architect of his day. The young Robert matured within this context of intense intellectual stimulation, and in 1743 he matriculated at the University of Edinburgh. But the dominant influences remained his father and his father's profession. Deeply influenced by James Gibbs and Colen Campbell, William Adam held the post of Master Mason in North Britain to the Board of Ordnance and worked for most of the Scottish peerage, from the duke of Hamilton down. Apart from his practical work, however, William Adam also had a scholarly side to his nature and compiled his designs for buildings into a publication called *Vitruvius Scoticus*, obviously patterned upon Campbell's seminal *Vitruvius Britannicus*. Robert Adam, the second son, joined his brothers in assisting their father with this volume and, of course, worked alongside them in the architectural office. After William Adam's death, in 1748, the two eldest sons, John and Robert, assumed control of the family business and completed the work begun by their father at Fort George and Hopetoun. Besides giving him valuable professional experience, these years as a practising architect strengthened Robert Adam's financial independence to the point where he was able to undertake his Grand Tour in 1754 with great comfort.

The importance and effect of Adam's years abroad

29. The Williams Wynn House. The second drawing room.

(October 1754–January 1758) have been discussed earlier. Travelling with sufficient means and in the company of Charles Hope, the younger brother of Lord Hopetoun, one of his Scottish patrons, Robert Adam found few doors closed to him. He met Cochin in France, Piranesi, Winckelmann, Mengs, Batoni and Gavin Hamilton in Italy, and in Rome had the good fortune of engaging the services of Charles Louis Clérisseau, one of the most accomplished architectural draughtsmen of his day and, in later years, architect to Catherine II of Russia. Clérisseau became Adam's friend and artistic *al factotum*, tutoring him in drawing, guiding him around the Italian antiquities and ruins and accompanying him to Spalato. During these years in the south, Robert Adam applied himself single mindedly to his studies of antique and Renaissance design, broadening, deepening, constantly refining the core of theoretical and applied knowledge which he had first developed in Scotland. When he returned to Britain, he came as a master of and authority on the classical world. His conception of his art and its relation to the antique were underpinned by a massive vocabulary of architectural detail, and there lay the seeds of the future Adam style.

A man of intense and driving ambition, Robert Adam established himself in London rather than return north. He made use of his Scottish connections and established contact with Lord Mansfield and Lord Bute, both of whom, in time, gave their countryman commissions. But, most effectively of all, Adam made the rounds of potential aristocratic patrons, showing them his designs, explaining his conceptions of decoration and establishing his reputation as a man of learning, taste and skill. Within a remarkably short time, these tactics brought success and commissions. In these early projects, we can see the as yet undeveloped elements which quickly came to mark all of Adam's work. In 1759 Admiral Edward Boscawen engaged Adam to decorate some rooms at Hatchlands. Compared to his later works, many aspects of these designs seem primi-

30. The Williams Wynn House. A detail from the principal front.

31. The Williams Wynn House. A detail from the dining room.

tive. The elements have a heaviness, a four square quality which seems more Palladian than Adam, the high relief stucco and widespread use of wood carving for decoration marking this clearly as an early work. The ceilings, on the other hand, were executed with a precision and delicacy that are also apparent in Adam's next important house, Shardeloes. Again, some elements, the heavy mahogany door for instance, seem out of place, but the disposition of the reception rooms *en suite* and the use of the doric order for the entrance hall, two typical Adam motifs, point unmistakeably to further developments of the mature style. As Adam carefully felt his way to this new mode of interior planning, he also experimented with furniture design. After some early efforts with the straight legs and simple forms of the *goût grec*, he abandoned, temporarily, this Neo-Classical path and played with designs which seemed more Rococo in temperament. But, however inconclusive and partly conceived some of these efforts may seem, these first few years were important for the establishment of Adam's reputation and the development of his unique style.

As Adam moved into the 1760's full blown success came quickly, almost effortlessly. Adam's appointment late in 1761 with William Chambers as joint architect to George III and the publication of the Spalato folio in 1764 only added to his renown. The 1760's were largely devoted to the completion and decoration of Adam's famous country house schemes, and his work at Syon, Kedleston, Kenwood, Harewood, Osterley and many others dates from this period. The rooms planned for these houses confirmed the tentative efforts of his earlier exercises. There is a coherence and uniformity of design, in a more general sense a careful harmonisation of details, which is missing at, say, Hatchlands. And the process of refinement continued. Adam lightened his stucco decoration, making it flatter and more linear. The heavy Palladian elements were weakened and made more classically simple in line and form. This process can be seen clearly at Syon House if the earlier ante-room is compared to the famous gallery completed in 1767. The high relief ceiling in the hall, the bulging half columns, simply the accentuated architectural detail and decoration of the ante-room, stunning as it is, were replaced by delicately described pilaster strips, gentle arabesque panel ornamentation and a linear, complex ceiling design in the gallery. Adam's furniture designs evolved similarly, and he returned to some of the more formal aspects of the *goût grec*. He totally adopted, at this point, the straight leg for his

32. The Williams Wynn House. Lady Williams Wynn's dressing room.

chairs and tables, and the process of refinement was also applied to mirrors, which lost their heavily ornamented frames in favour of narrower ones emphasizing the rectangular shape of the glass. At this time Adam also minimised his use of carved wood for decoration in favour of the more elegant ormolu, a gold coloured alloy of copper, zinc and tin. Delicate strings of ormolu beads were used to outline pilasters, column fluting and bases and mantelpieces, a stylistic development which furthered the lightness which increasingly characterised his work.

Adam's responsibilities at these country houses varied from commission to commission. At the Dashwood seat of West Wycombe, he designed only stables and kitchens and perhaps the west portico, but at Kedleston he was entrusted with the completion of the south façade and the decoration of the rooms. This is not the place for a detailed examination of all of Adam's projects, but some of his most famous masterpieces must not be neglected. At Syon, Adam triumphed over the demands of a house existing since the fifteenth century. Using such devices as columnar screens he modified mis-shapen rooms to fit symmetrical and classical standards, and, through the careful use of steps, linked rooms which had been built on slightly different levels. The duke of Northumberland, the owner of Syon, ultimately called a halt to Adam's expenditure, but the great domed hall, planned for the central court, though unexecuted at Syon, appeared transformed in other Adam plans. Kedleston provided one of Adam's few opportunities to work with exterior elevations, and his use of the triumphal Arch of Constantine as the leading motif was a perfect Neo-Classical solution. The saloon of Kedleston was planned as a circle, a shape which

33. The Williams Wynn House. The music room.

34. Home House. The music room.

Adam used again for the saloon at Culzean Castle. Osterley remains one of Adam's most striking efforts and displays his facility at grafting eighteenth century modes onto earlier structures, in this case a double portico derived from the Portico of Octavia, embedded as an entrance into an Elizabethan building. The ceiling of the music room at Harewood may be taken as typical of Adam's ceiling designs; a central star was placed in a circle and surrounded by swags, paterae and medallions painted by Angelica Kauffmann. This pattern of decoration for ceilings and walls appeared in nearly all Adam designed houses, and the motifs of swags, paterae, painted medallions, anthemion devices, arabesques, sphinxes and fans, used in constantly varying combinations, formed an important part of the legacy from the years abroad. Perhaps the quintessential Adam design, however, was that for the library of Lord Mansfield at Kenwood. It contains many of the elements characteristic of the Adam style: apsidial endings screened by corinthian columns, a chimney piece and mirror wall combination, and above all, a vaulted ceiling with his favourite tripartite compartmentation and decorated with painted medallions and low relief stucco work.

At the same time that Adam's artistic style became increasingly refined, his personal life established itself into the pattern it was to maintain for the rest of his life. The Adam family was extremely close-knit. Very few of William Adam's ten children married, Robert included, and most of them seemed content to lead a life centred around the talented brother who was making his name in London. Two of the sisters moved south to manage Robert's household for him, and after his return from the Grand Tour, James Adam joined this family compound. James played an extremely important role in his brother's life and was a more than

35. Shelburne House. The dining room.

competent architect in his own right, but his relationship to Robert is clearly delineated in a humorous passage from a letter James wrote on the continent. "You may assure Bob, I shall pardon him for superior merit. I am much less ambitious than Caesar, I am contented to hold a second place." And despite the credit James shared with Robert in the full title of *The Works*, there can be little doubt that the younger brother's career was subservient to that of the elder. He helped Robert with his projects, sometimes as a collaborator but more often as an assistant, and undertook very few designs on his own. It is hardly surprising that this intense degree of almost dynastic solidarity extended into business, for while Robert and James designed buildings and interiors from London, the youngest brother, William, managed the finances of the firm, and the eldest, John, looked after the family interests in the north from the patrimony of Blair-Adam. When Adam Bros. began a massive venture, as the Adelphi, it was very much a family undertaking.

The construction of the complex of buildings which the Adams called the Adelphi (appropriately derived from the Greek word for "brothers") consumed six years (1768–1774) and underlined several trends which distinguished the 1770's from the decade which preceded them. For one, it pointed to the increasingly urban orientation of Robert Adam's work. Whereas many of his commissions in the 1760's were for country houses,

36. The Williams Wynn House. A stucco panel from the music room.

37. Shelburne House. The principal front.

38. Shelburne House. The porter's hall.

39. Shelburne House. The ceiling of the drawing room.

the great town houses in Portman Square, Grosvenor Square, Berkeley Square and Queen Anne Street all date from the '70's. The Adelphi was Adam's most ambitious urban scheme and resulted, at least in part, from the failure of the state to provide a public commission of what he considered to be suitable proportions. In 1768 the Adam brothers leased the site of Durham Yard, on the north bank of the Thames, from the duke of St Albans. They embanked and drained the Thames river edge and began erecting Robert's ambitious plans for contiguous town houses, one row, the Royal Terrace, facing the river, with another parallel behind it and two more rows perpendicular to the river. Some observers found the Adelphi façades excessively plain and simple. The lateral blocks projected a bit further towards the Thames than the Royal Terrace and thus formed almost terminal pavilions, an understated example of Adam's concept of "movement", while the main block itself was punctuated with only slight projections and slender, ornamental pilasters. Notwithstanding Horace Walpole's dismissal of the design as looking like a soldier's trull tarted up in the regimental braid, competition for houses and shops in the Adelphi was keen. Adam himself occupied No. 4, next door to his close friend, David Garrick. But despite the popularity of the Adelphi, the undertaking pushed the entire and previously prosperous Adam firm and family to the brink of bankruptcy. By 1772 the brothers owed £140,000 because of the Adelphi venture, and David Hume estimated that each year of building would add £100,000 to this sum. The decision of the government not to lease the underground vaults in the Adelphi for storage exacerbated the problem, and it was only through recourse to a public lottery that the Adams managed to extricate themselves from disaster. The financial difficulties of the Adelphi and a rather unseemly law suit over stucco patents, adjudged (1778) in Robert Adam's favour by his friend and client, Lord Mansfield, tarnished the reputation of the firm. There were other disappointments as well, including the col-

40. Culzean Castle. The drawing room.

lapse of Robert's plans for the development of Portland Place. Increased competition also caused concern, especially that of James Wyatt in architectural planning and Thomas Chippendale and John Linnell in furniture design. All three were strongly influenced by the established Adam style, and their growing popularity came just at the time that the Adams saw the circle of patronage contracting because of financial pressure. The American War, which began in 1775, discouraged property developers and speculators from investing in buildings, and James Adam wrote that the "long continuance and vast expanse of the American War by checking the national ardour for the fine arts procured me opportunities of attending" to his subsidiary pastime, agriculture.

But despite these setbacks and disappointments, the 1770's were not devoid of achievement. Robert Adam was elected the Member of Parliament for Kinross-shire in 1768, serving until the Parliament of 1774, and although he rarely spoke in the house and generally followed the lead of Lord Bute and Lord Mansfield, this post gave him the opportunity of making useful business contacts. Also, in 1773 the first instalment of *The Works in Architecture of Robert and James Adam* appeared. Whether it was conceived as an advertising ploy to bolster what the brothers feared was a flagging patronage or as a celebration of their own considerable achievement, this volume was a worthy successor to Robert Adam's earlier work on Spalato. Indeed, many of the artists who had engraved for Adam before were employed again, including Cunego, Bartolozzi and Zucchi, while the standard was raised even more by the inclusion of four Piranesi prints. The early and relatively immature designs, such as those for Hatchlands and Shardeloes, were not included in this collection, and Adam illustrated only what he considered to be his best

41. Culzean Castle. The oval staircase.

42. The Register House of Scotland. The principal front.

plans, elevations and designs for furniture. In one way, the publication of *The Works* fell into a family tradition and was a filial continuation of *Vitruvius Scoticus*, devoted to the designs of the senior William Adam. A second volume appeared in 1779, and a third was published posthumously in 1822.

There was also the succession of distinguished town houses which kept the Adam firm busy and added to Robert's stature during the 1770's. As at Syon, Adam was required to cope with problems which might have baffled a lesser architect, in these cases the limitations of the restricted size and dimensions of plots in London's fashionable squares. The exteriors of most of these houses are restrained and dignified exercises, with discreet, unaccented windows, and, as usual, Adam lavished most of his inventive genius on the interiors, where he managed to compensate for the lack of space with his customary ingenuity. Specific patterns and solutions appear again and again during any investigation of Adam's town houses. He habitually paid especially careful attention to the hall and staircase composition, usually the first view which faced a visitor to the house, and managed to make these volumes seem more spacious and extended than they really are. By varying the sizes and shapes of the reception rooms, usually arranged *en suite* as in the country houses, Adam avoided the monotony seemingly inherent in much of urban interior design. One of the finest of the town houses produced by Adam was the one built for Sir Watkin Williams Wynn at No. 20 St James's Square. The exquisite stairwell, enriched with the expected Adam motifs of anthemion, arabesques and winged lions, is typical of the Adam mode and extends the full height of the hall, although the main staircase, as usual, leads only to the first floor rooms. The staircase itself is a masterpiece of iron balustrade and mahogany hand-

43. The Register House of Scotland. A detail from the ceiling of the dome.

rail. The Williams Wynn house is also important because it contains one of Adam's finest rooms. The first floor drawing room, with its compartmented, vaulted ceiling, medallion decoration and semi-domes at both ends, clearly is a first cousin to the library at Kenwood. Similarly, No. 20 Portman Square, executed for the countess of Home, demonstrates Adam's unique gifts with stairwells. In this house, Adam, using a staircase remarkably similar to that at the Williams Wynn house, manipulated the stairs in a circular well with the central flight dividing at a half-landing into two lesser branches leading to the first floor. The Portman Square house also contains one of the few surviving examples of Adam's Etruscan style, with an entire room treated in the colour scheme of cream-white, black and ochre (or Pompeian red). Adam also used this Etruscan mode in his sumptuous designs for Derby House in Grosvenor Square, where the segmented cross-vault of the ground floor parlour seems to have been derived from the Villa Madama, another example of Adam's debt to the Renaissance.

Stylistically, the 1770's saw an intensification and progression of the Adam mode of the 1760's. The process of refinement and attenuation of detail reached a high point in the music room of Home House, where the thinnest of pilaster strips support a weightless entablature with an all but non-existent cornice. The decoration became, if anything, flatter and lighter than before and totally generalised in its application to surfaces. Adam's treatment of furniture proceeded along identical lines. Tables were reduced to a thin frieze supported by narrow legs, and the mirrors were surrounded by even more restrained frames, the surface of the glass often decorated with delicate patterns in ormolu. None

44. The Register House of Scotland. The interior of the dome.

of this furniture had an accent of its own, but instead was designed to be completely subservient to a total scheme. The Adam style reached fruition in the 1770's, and Horace Walpole's carping analysis of it as "all gingerbread, filigraine, and fan painting" should not obscure its extreme gracefulness and elegance and the staggering harmonisation of every element in every Adam room.

During the 1780's, the last full decade of Robert Adam's life, his career proceeded in a different direction, not stylistically as much as geographically. Obviously, Adam's roots always remained in London. He continued to live in the capital and to accept English commissions. He carefully maintained his London contacts and in 1791, with James Wyatt, George Dance, Sir William Chambers, Henry Holland, John Sloane and John Yenn among others, founded the Architect's Club, which, in time, became the Royal Institute of British Architects. But increasingly during the 1780's Robert Adam found himself engaged in activities in his native Scotland, and a great deal of time was spent in commuting north of the Tweed, not an easy process in the eighteenth century. Some of these Scottish commissions came from private patrons and provided opportunities for Adam to experiment with the increasingly popular Gothic style, which undoubtedly appealed to the Romantic inclinations apparent in the Salvator Rosa-esque landscape sketches he made at this time. His domestic masterpiece of this period was the work he undertook for the earl of Cassilis at Culzean Castle on the Ayrshire coast. The battlemented façade is so romanticised in design that it is reminiscent of one of Inigo Jones's masque drawings. The grandly Gothic exterior, however, was wedded to an interior of impeccable Neo-Classical origins. The magnificent staircase was adorned with all of the three Greek orders, but, typically with Adam, their traditional order was rearranged; the doric was used for the ground floor while the corinthian and ionic surround the first and second floor landings respectively. The circular saloon, overlooking the sea, was another triumph for Adam, with the concentric circles of the carpet and ceiling designs balancing and complementing each other, yet another of Adam's favourite methods for harmonising the components of a room.

Stimulating as this work for Scottish nobles was, most of Adam's activity centred upon Edinburgh, where, at last, it seemed he would receive the string of large scale, public commissions for which he had hoped. The Adam family had been associated with the building of classical Edinburgh from the beginning, and John Adam, the eldest brother, had been one of the designers of the North Bridge, which linked the Old Town to the New. From the 1770's the Edinburgh municipal authorities turned increasingly to Robert Adam for advice and plans. The monumental, almost Palladian Register House was designed as early as 1772, although not completed until over twenty years later. Its gently rising dome is reminiscent of the domed central halls which Adam planned for Syon House and Luton Park House. In the 1780's he was deluged by commissions for the Scottish capital. His South Bridge was opened in 1788, and by 1791 he had designed the whole of Charlotte Square for the New Town. He was also entrusted with laying out Queen Street and in 1785 was asked to design a new university. Gratifying as these projects must have been, the 1780's were not easy for Adam. In nearly all his schemes and plans for Edinburgh, he was faced with the stalling tactics if not the outright opposition of Edinburgh officialdom. The South Bridge was delayed month after month, and it was only with the aid of his cousin, William Robertson, the principal of the University of Edinburgh, that Adam's scheme of

45. The University of Edinburgh. The courtyard front with the dome (1875) of Sir Rowand Anderson.

47. The University of Edinburgh. A detail of the east front.

46. The University of Edinburgh. The east front with the dome (1875) of Sir Rowand Anderson.

a double quadrangle was accepted and begun upon. Shortages of money, labour disputes, official hostility which often took the form of petty intrusions into Adam's work, all complicated, impeded, retarded his activities. Then, in 1792, came the greatest tragedy, for on 3 March Robert Adam died suddenly from a stomach haemorrhage. Of all Adam's major public commissions for Edinburgh, only the South Bridge was finished in his lifetime, although the Register House was close to completion. The death of James Adam in 1794 removed the only other person to whom the authentic and accurate execution of Robert's designs could have been entrusted with any assurance, and the long term commitment to wars with revolutionary and Napoleonic France discouraged building activity for nearly twenty years. When Adam's Edinburgh schemes were finally realised in the early nineteenth century, they emerged altered and reduced by other architects, and even though his ideas were an important basis for the evolution of Edinburgh as we know it today, the Athens of the North reflects more the dour, solid outlook of such craftsmen as Robert Reid and William Playfair than it does the classical vision of Robert Adam.

In some ways Robert Adam's career seems remarkably parallel to that of a man he attacked as a purveyor of Palladianism, Inigo Jones. Both were native born British artists who ripened their sensitivities during tours of Italy, both forged elements of the antique and *cinquecento* styles into unique personal visions and both returned to Britain and helped to effect a total revolution in the style and taste of their own times. Robert Adam was certainly one of the most important British Neo-Classicists, and the changes which he brought about in design can be seen as a major contribution to the acceptance of this style. Yet, on another level, his achievement lies in his role as the liberator of architecture and design from what had become merely ossified standards of procedure. His reliance upon and firm faith in the intuition and genius of the individual artist marked his style as one of the most uniquely personal and elegant statements in the history of British art and architecture.

THE PREFACES
AND
EXPLANATIONS
OF THE
PLATES

A Student conducted to Minerva, who points to Greece and Italy, as the Countries from where he must derive the most perfect Knowledge and Taste in elegant Architecture. Frontispiece (dated 1775) to The Works in Architecture of Robert and James Adam. *Engraved by Francesco Bartolozzi after Antonio Zucchi.*

THE

WORKS IN ARCHITECTURE

OF

ROBERT AND JAMES ADAM, ESQUIRES.

VOLUME I.

Containing the Five following NUMBERS, viz.

I. The SEAT of the DUKE of NORTHUMBERLAND, at SION.

II. The VILLA of EARL MANSFIELD, at KENWOOD.

III. The SEAT of the EARL of BUTE, at LUTON PARK.

IV. PUBLIC BUILDINGS.

V. DESIGNS for the KING and QUEEN, and the PRINCESS DOWAGER of WALES, &c.

LONDON: Printed for the AUTHORS;

And ſold by PETER ELMSLY, oppoſite Southampton Street in the Strand, and by the other Bookſellers in Town and Country.

MDCCLXXVIII.

I

PREFACE.

SOME apology may, perhaps, be requiſite, for giving to the world a book of architecture, after ſo many works of this kind have been publiſhed in Italy, France and England during the tow laſt centuries.

The novelty and variety of the following deſigns, will, we flatter ourſelves, not only excuſe, but justify our conduct, in communicating them to the world.------ We have not trod in the path of others, nor derived aid from their labours. In the works which we have had the honour to execute, we have not only met with the approbation of our employers, but even with the imitation of other artiſts, to ſuch a degree, as in ſome meaſure to have brought about, in this country; a kind of revolution in the whole ſyſtem of this uſeful and elegant art. Theſe circumſtances induced us to hope, that to collect and engrave our works would afford both entertainment and inſtruction.

To enter upon an enquiry into the ſtate of this art in Great Britain, till the late changes it has undergone, is no part of our preſent deſign. We leave that ſubject to the obſervation of the ſkilful; who we doubt not, will eaſily perceive, within theſe few years, a remarkable improvement in the form, convenience, arrangement, and relief of apartments; a greater movement (A) and variety, in the outſide compoſition, and in the decoration of the inſide, an almoſt total change.

The maſſive entablature (B), the ponderous compartment ceiling (C), the tabernacle frame, almoſt the only ſpecies of ornament (D) formerly known, in this country, are now univerſally exploded, and in their place, we have adopted a beautiful variety of light mouldings, gracefully formed, delicately enriched and arranged with propriety and ſkill. We have introduced a great diverſity of ceilings, freezes, and decorated pilaſters, and have added grace and beauty to the whole, by a mixture of groteſque (E) ſtucco, and painted ornaments, together with the flowing rainceau (F), with its fanciful figures and winding foliage.

Whether our works have not contributed to diffuſe theſe improvements in architecture, through this country, we ſhall leave to the impartial public. — We, by no means, preſume to find fault, with the compoſitions, or to decry the labours of other authors; many of whom have much merit and deſerve great praiſe. Our ambition is to ſhare with others, not to appropriate to ourſelves the applauſe of the public; and, if we have any claim to approbation, we found it on this alone : That we flatter ourſelves, we have been able to ſeize, with ſome degree of ſucceſs, the beautiful ſpirit of antiquity, and to transfuſe it, with novelty and variety, through all our numerous works.

We intended to have prefixed to our deſigns a diſſertation concerning the riſe and progreſs of architecture in Great Britain; and to have pointed out the various ſtages of its improvements from the time, that our anceſtors, relinquiſhingn the gothick ſtyle, began to aim at an imitation of the Grecian manner, until it attained that degree of perfection at which it has now arrived. — We have made many obſervations, and collcted various materials to enable us to illuſtrate this curious and entertaining ſubject; but to digeſt and arrange theſe would require more time than we can command amidſt the multiplied occupations of an active profeſſion. We, therefore, reſerve the ſubject for ſome period of greater leiſure.

The rules and orders of architecture, are ſo generally known, and may be found in ſo many books, that it would be tedious, and even abſurd, to treat of them in this work. We beg leave, however, to obſerve that among architects deſtitute of genius and incapable of venturing into the great line of their art, the attention paid to thoſe rules and proportions is frequently minute and frivolous. The great maſters of antiquity were not so rigidly ſcrupulous, they varied the proportions as the general ſpirit of their compoſition required, clearly perceiving, that however neceſſary theſe rules may be to form the taſte and to correct the licentiouſneſs of the ſcholar, they often cramp the genius and circumſcribe the ideas of the maſter.

We have given a ſhort explanation of the plates, accompanied with ſuch obſervations as we imagined might be both uſeful entertaining.

We have thought it proper to colour with the tints, uſed in the execution, a few copies of each number, not only that poſterity might be enabled to judge with more accuracy concerning the taſte of the preſent age, and that foreign connoiſſeurs might have it in their power to indulge their curioſity with reſpect to our national ſtyle of ornament; but that the public in general might have an opportunity of cultivating the beautiful art of decoration, hitherto ſo little underſtood in moſt of the countries of Europe.

We hope it will be thought no more than juſtice to ourſelves, thus to aſcertain the originality of our deſigns. and enable the world to diſcover, where they have been imitated with judgment, and where they have been ſervilely copied or miſapplied.------An artiſt who feels in himſelf an inability of preſenting to the public any thing from his own ſtore of invention, has no title to be offended if an author is ſolicitous to vindicate himſelf to poſterity from any imputation of plagiariſm.

As this work will not only exhibit deſigns in architecture, but alſo in every kind of ornamental furniture, we imagine it may be particularly uſeful to thoſe whoſe profeſſions require taſte and elegance in that way.

(A) *Movement* is meant to expreſs, the riſe and fall, the advance and receſs, with other diverſity of form, in the different parts of a building, ſo as to add greatly to the picturesque of the compoſition. For the riſing and falling, advancing and receding, with the convexity and concavity, and other forms of the great parts, have the ſame effect in architecture, that hill and dale, fore-ground and diſtance, ſwelling and ſinking have in lanſcape : That is, they ſerve to produce an agreeable and diverſified contour, that groups and contraſts like a picture, and creates a variety of light and ſhade, which gives great ſpirit, beauty and effect to the compoſition.

It is not always that ſuch variety can be introduced into the deſign of any building but where it can be attained without encroaching upon its uſeful purpoſes, it adds much to its merit, as an object of beauty and grandeur.

The effect of the height and convexity of the dome of St. Peter's, contraſted with the lower ſquare front, and the concavity of its court, is a ſtriking inſtance of this ſort of compoſition. The college and church *des quatre nations* at Paris, is though ſmall, another of the ſame kind; and with us, we really do not recollect any example of ſo much movement and contraſt, as in the ſouth front of Kedleſton houſe in Derbyſhire, one of the ſeats of the Right Honourable Lord Scarſdale, of which building we ſhall have occaſion to ſpeak more at large hereafter.

We cannot however allow ourſelves to cloſe this note without doing juſtice to the memory of a great man, whoſe reputation as an architect, has been long carried down the ſtream by a torrent of undiſtinguiſhing prejudice and abuſe.

Sir John Vanburgh's genius was of the firſt claſs; and, in point of movement, novelty and ingenuity, his works have not been exceeded by any thing in modern times. We ſhould certainly have quoted Blenheim and Caſtle Howard as great examples of theſe perfections, in preference to any work of our own, or of any other modern architect; but unluckily for the reputation of this excellent artiſt, his taſte kept no pace with his genius, and his works are ſo crouded with barbariſms and abſurdities, and ſo borne down by their own prepofterous weight, that none but the difcerning can feparate their merits from their defects. In the hands of the ingenious artift, who knows how to polifh and refine and bring them into ufe, we have always regarded his productions, as rough jewels of ineftimable value.

(B) *The maffive entablature.* It is well known to every one who has made architecture, in any degree, the object of his attention, that the entablature conftitutes a principal part or each order, and is itfelf formed of three great divifions, the architrave, freeze and cornice.

It is not here meant to find fault with the whole, or its component parts, but fo far only as it has been abused by the mifapplication, ignorance, and want of invention in many modern artifts.

Nothing can be more noble and ftriking, when properly applied, than a fine order of columns, with their bafes, capitals, and entablatures : nothing more fterile and difguftful, than to fee for ever the dull repetition of Dorick, Ionick, and Corinthian entablatures, in their ufual proportions, reigning round every apartment, where no order can come or ought to come; and yet it is aftonifhing to think that this has been almoft invariably the cafe in the apartments of every houfe in Europe, that has any pretenfions to magnificence, from the days of Bramante down to our time. In fmaller rooms, where height is wanting, the architrave has fometimes been omitted, and fometimes both architrave and freeze, but their places were ponderoufly fupplied by a cornice of moft ample dimenfions fit for the temple of Jupiter Tonans, from which it was imitated perhaps, or, more probably, copied.

To defcribe here in what manner this tirefome repetition may be avoided, would be, to anticipate the purpofe of the prefent work, which, among other things, is intended to point out a new ftile of compofition for thofe parts of interior decoration.

(C) *Compartment ceiling;* a name given to all ceilings that are divided into various pannels, furrounded with mouldings, a mode to which we do not here mean to object, there being many beautiful compofitions of this kind, both ancient and modern; but the epithet of *ponderous* is applied to diftnguifh thofe that were in ufe in this country, during the laft century, from thofe of the prefent times; the ftile of the former being of a moft enormous weight and depth.

Thefe abfurd compofitions took their rife in Italy, under the firft of their modern mafters, who were no doubt led into that idea from the obfervations of the soffits ufed by the ancients in the porticos of their temples and other public works. Thefe the ancients, with their ufual fkill and judgement, kept of a bold and maffive ftyle, fuiting them to the ftrength, magnitude, and height of the building, and making an allowance for their being on the exterior part, and adjoining to other great objects; all which ferved to diminifh and lighten the effect to thefe compartments. — But on the infide of their edifices the ancients were extremely careful to proportion both the fize and depth of their compartments and pannels, to the diftance from the eye and the objects with which they were to be compared; and, with regard to the decoration of their private and bathing apartments, they were all delicacy, gaiety, grace, and beauty. If the reader is defirous to examine more minutely into thefe truths, let him confult the Rotunda, the Temple of Peace, the ruins of Adrian's villa, the Palace of the Emperors, and other Cryptæ at Rome, with the inimitable remains on the Baian fhore. — We fhall only add, that from this miftake of the firft modern Italian artifts, all Europe has been mifled, and has been fervilely groaning under this load for thefe three centuries paft.

Michael Angelo, Raphael, Pyrro Ligerio, Dominichino, Georgio Vafari, and Algardi, with great tafte and knowledge, threw off thefe prejudices, and boldly aimed at reftoring the antique.

But at this time the rage of painting became fo prevalent in Italy, that inftead of following thefe great examples, they covered every ceiling with large fresco compofitions, which, tho' extremely fine and well painted, were very much mifplaced, and muft neceffarily, from the attitude in which they are beheld, tire the patience of every fpectator. Great compofitions fhould be placed fo as to be viewed with eafe. Grotefque ornaments and figures, in any fituation, are perceived with the glance of an eye, and require little examination.

The heavy compartment ceilings were afterwards adopted in France; and Le Potre adorned them with all the trappings of his luxuriant imagination. Inigo Jones introduced them into England, with as much weight, but lefs fancy and embellifhment.

Vanburgh, Campbell, and Gibbs, followed too implicitly the authority of this great name. Kent's genius for the picturefque, and the vaft reputation he defervedly acquired, made him in fome meafure withftand this prevalent abufe; he has much merit in being the firft who began to lighten his compartments, and to introduce grotefque paintings with his ornaments in ftucco. His works, however, are evidently thofe of a beginner. Mr. Stuart, with his ufual elegance and tafte has contributed greatly towards introducing the true ftyle of antique decoration; and it feems to have been referved for the prefent times to fee compartment ceilings, and thofe of every kind, carried to a degree of perfection in Great Britain, that far furpaffes any of the former attempts of other modern nations.

(D) *Tabernacle Frame;* a collective term, made ufe of by Englifh artifts to exprefs the whole dreffing of a door, window, nich, or chimney, when the dreffing confifts of columns or pilafters with an entablature and pediment over them. This term feems not to have been borrowed from the Latin, Italian, or French, the ufual fources from whence our technical phrafes flow. We are therefore of opinion, that it has taken its rife in this country from the general cuftom of decorating all the altar-pieces of our churches in this ftyle.

In Roman catholic countries, that part of the altar where the cup containing the Hoft is placed, is called tabernacle; and by an eafy tranfition, from a part to the whole, we have given the altar-piece the name of tabernacle.

This piece of decoration, which is extremely noble and beautiful, when well compofed, is only condemned from its mifapplication and frequent repetition in infide finifhing, where it is by much too heavy and bold to admit of the gay and the elegant, unlefs in very great apartments.

(E) By *grotefque* is meant that beautiful light ftile of ornament ufed by the ancient Romans, in the decoration of their palaces, baths and villas. It is alfo to be feen in fome of their amphitheatres, temples and tombs; the greateft part of which being vaulted and covered with ruins, have been dug up and cleared by the modern Italians, who for thefe reafons, give them the name of *grotte*, which is perhaps a corruption of the Latin *Griptæ*, a word borrowed from the Greeks, as the Romans did moft of their terms in architecture; and hence the modern word *grotefque*, and the Englifh word *grotto*, fignifying a cave.

In the times of Raphael, Michael Angelo, Julio Romano, Polidoro, Giov. d'Udine, Vafari, Zuchero and Algardi, there is no doubt but there was much greater remains of the grotte, than what are now to be feen, and in imitation of them, were decorated the loggias of the Vatican, the villas Madama, Pamfili, Caprarola, the old palace at Florence; and indeed whatever elfe is elegant or admirable in the finifhings of modern Italy. The French, who till of late never adopted the ornaments of the ancients, and jealous as all mankind are of the reputation of their national tafte, have branded thofe ornaments with the vague and fantaftical appellation of arabefque, a ftile which, though entirely diftinct from the grotefque, has, notwithftanding, been moft abfurdly and univerfally confounded with it by the ignorant.

This claffical ftile of ornament, by far the moft perfect that has ever appeared for infide decorations, and which has ftood the teft of many ages, like other works of genius, requires not only fancy and imagination in the compofition, but tafte and judgement in the application; and when thefe are happily combined, this gay and elegant mode is capable of inimitable beauties.

Vitruvius with great reafon condemns an over licentioufnefs in compofitions of this kind, and blames the painters of his time for introducing monftrous extravagancies. We mean not to vindicate any thing that deferves fuchs appellations but furely in light and gay compofitions, defigned merely to amufe, it is not altogether neceffary to exclude the whimfical and the bifarre.

(F) *Rairçeau*, apparently derived from *rain*, an old French word, fignifying the branch of a tree. This French term is alfo ufed by the artifts of this country, to exprefs the winding and twifting of the ftalk or ftem of the acanthus plant; which flowing round in many graceful turnings, fpreads its foliage with great beauty and variety, and is often intermixed, with human figures, animals and birds, imaginary or real; alfo with flowers and fruits.

This gay and fanciful diverfity of agreeable objects, well compofed, and delicately executed in ftucco of painting, attains a wonderfull power of pleafing.

We hope this minute explanation of thefe terms will be excufed. It is intended to fupply in fome meafure a geneal deficiency which we have found upon this fubject, in all the encyclopedias and technical dictionaries.

PLANS of SION HOUSE,

FROM THE

DESIGNS of ROBERT ADAM.

IN the year 1762, the Duke of Northumberland came to the refolution of fitting up the apartments of Sion House, in a magnificent manner. He communicated his intentions to me, and having expreffed his defire, that the whole might be executed intirely in the antique ftyle, he was pleafed, in terms very flattering, to fignify his confidence in my abilities to follow out his idea.

Upon this plan, the alterations and infide decorations of Sion House were begun, and as the idea was to me a favourite one, the fubject great, the expence unlimited, and the Duke himfelf a person of extenfive knowledge and correct tafte in architecture, I endeavoured to render it a noble and elegant habitation, not unworthy of a proprietor, who poffeffed not only wealth to execute a great defign, but skill to judge of its merit.

Some inequality in the levels on the old floors, fome limitations from the fituation of the old walls, and fome want of additional heights to the enlarged apartments, were the chief difficulties with which I had to ftruggle. Thefe difficulties I flatter myfelf are in a great meafure furmounted, fo as not only to procure much convenience in the arrangement of the apartments, but likewife an elegant form and graceful proportion in the principal rooms.

The inequality of levels has been managed in fuch a manner as to increafe the fcenery and add to the movement, fo that an apparent defect has been converted into a real beauty.

EXPLANATION of the PLATES.

PLATE I.

Plan and elevation of the GATEWAY *and* PORTERS-LODGES, *fronting the great weft road.*

The collonade and iron rail underneath, not only give an air of magnificence to this building, but were alfo intended by His Grace to gratify the curiofity of the public, by giving to travellers an opportunity of viewing from the road, the park, lawn, bridge, river, and the houfe itfelf at a little diftance, clofing the beautiful fcene.

An infcription was propofed on the pannel over the gateway. The lyon on the pedeftal at top is the ancient creft of the Percys.

PLATE II.

Detail, or parts at large of the GATEWAY *fronting the great weft road.*

This detail will be found to have novelty, and I hope fome degree of beauty to recommend it. The capital is altogether new, and has been deemed not unpleafing. The lyon's head introduced on the abbacus, and alfo in the center of the patera, and the claws, which whimfically form the bafes of the pilafters, allude to the Percy creft.

The crefcent introduced in the entablature and body of the vafe, is the prefent creft of the family. The vafe itfelf is of a graceful form, and the iron rail that runs between the columns is ftrong, yet light and uncommon.

PLATE III.

Plan and elevation of the BRIDGE *over a branch of the river Thames.*

This bridge makes part of the way leading from the great gate to the houfe; and I have endeavoured to make the decoration, light, gay, and graceful, the ideas which naturally arife in beholding the adjacent fcenes. The whole is new, and is reckoned fanciful and pictorefque.

To fuit a building to a fcene, requires not only tafte, but judgment in an artift. If any one fhall copy this bridge, it muft be placed neither in a deep valley, nor over a navigable river.

PLATE IV.

Perspective view of the fame BRIDGE.

PLATE V.

Plan of the principal FLOOR *of Sion House.*

What is fhaded dark is already executed, what is of a lighter tint fhows the alterations and additions ftill intended. The floor of the hall is confiderably lower than that of the other apartments; this feeming defect was entirely removed, by introducing a few fteps in the different places marked in the plan, which, as I have before obferved, has a happy effect, and gives an additional pictorefque to the fcene.

This plan, as it is here difpofed, affords an opportunity of making fome obfervations upon the form, arrangement, and relief of apartments, circumftances, which, however material, with refpect to elegance as well as ufe, have hitherto been extremely little underftood, or attended to, even in the greateft houfes of this country.

Variety and gracefulnefs of form, fo particularly courted by the ancients, have not been objects of much attention to modern artifts. Bramante, Raphael, and Michael Angelo, thofe great reftorers of the arts, almoft entirely neglected this pleafing fource of beauty. Pyrro Ligorio in his Papa Giulio and lodge in the Vatican garden, and fome few mafters of the Roman school, excited by the example of the ancients, and by an admiration of thofe remains of their works, which were always before their eyes, made fome feeble efforts to revive this elegant mode, which fince their time has been but little cultivated by Paladio, Jones, or any of the celebrated mafters of this art; and it is only of late, that it has been again introduced into Great Britain with fome rays of its ancient fplendor.

A proper arrangement and relief of apartments are branches of architecture in which the French have èxcelled all other nations : thefe have united magnificence with utility in the hotels of their nobility, and have rendered them objects of univerfal imitation.

To underftand thoroughly the art of living, it is neceffary, perhaps, to have paffed fome time amongft the French, and to have ftudied the cuftoms of that focial and converfible people. In one particular, however, our manners prevent us from imitating them. Their eating rooms feldom or never conftitute a piece in their great apartments, but lie out of the fuite, and in fitting them up, little attention is paid to beauty of decoration. The reafon of this is obvious; the French meet there only at meals, when they truft to the difplay of the table for fhow and magnificence, not to the decoration of the apartment; and as foon as the entertainment is over, they immediately retire to the rooms of company. It is not fo with us. Accuftomed by habit, or induced by the nature of our climate, we indulge more largely in the enjoyment of the bottle. Every perfon of rank here is either a membre of the legiflation, or entitled by his condition to take part in the political arrangements of his country, and to enter with ardour into thofe difcuffions to which they give rife; thefe circumftances lead men to live more with one another, and more detached from the fociety of the ladies. The eating rooms are confidered as the apartments of converfation, in which we are to pafs a great part of our time. This renders it defireable to have them fitted up with elegance and fplendor, but in a ftyle different from that of other apartments. Inftead of being hung with damafk, tapeftry, &c. they are always finifhed with ftucco, and adorned with ftatues and paintings, that they may not retain the fmell of the victuals.

But leaving a digreffion, which perhaps may appear not uninftructive, as it points out the neceffity of varying the ftyle of architecture fo as to accommodate it to the manners and habits of different nations, we fhall now return to a more regular infpection and explanation of the plan before us.

The hall, both in our houfes and in thofe of France, is a fpacious apartment, intended as the room of accefs where fervants in livery attend. It is here a room of great dimenfion, is finifhed with ftucco, as halls always are, and is formed with a recefs at each end, one fquare and the other circular, which have a noble effect and increafe the variety.

The anti-rooms on each fide, are for the attendance of the fervants out of livery, and alfo for that of tradefmen, &c. thefe are relieved by the back ftairs in the towers. That on the fide of the great apartment is fquare, and is decorated with columns of verd antique marble, as reprefented in the plan and fections, which ftanding infulated, ferve to form the room and heighten the fcenery. The anti-room, on the fide of the private apartment, is formed into an oval, a figure feldom or never ufed by the ancients, but has been fometimes introduced by the moderns with fuccefs, and was here in fome recpect neceffary from the oblong fhape of the room.

Next to the anti-rooms, are the public and private eating-rooms, the publick one is a room of great extent, finifhed with ftucco, and adorned with niches and ftatues of marble; it is formed into a great circular recefs at each end, decorated with fcreens of columns. The private one has alfo its receffes and ftucco finifhing, and is relieved by a back-ftair for the ufe of the fervants.

Next to the great eating-room, lies a fplendid with-drawing room, for the ladies, or falle de compagnie, as it is called by the French; this is varied from the other rooms, by the forms of its ceiling, which is coved and painted in compartments. It gives accefs into a gallery of great length, tho'rather too narrow and too low to be in the juft proportion we could have wifhed. It is, however, finifhed in a ftyle to afford great variety and amufement; and is, for this reafon, an admirable room for the reception of company before dinner, or for the ladies to retire to after it : For the with-drawing room lying between this and the eating room, prevents the noife of the men from being troublefome; and for this reafon, we would always recommend the intervention of a room, in great apartments, to prevent fuch inconvenience.

The little clofets or cabinets, the one circular for china, and the other fquare for miniatures, at each end of the gallery, ferve only for an additional amufement. The gallery itfelf, as well as the private apartments, is relieved by the circular back ftairs, and gives accefs to the ranges of apartments on both fides.

The great circular faloon, is a noble room, entering from the hall, and leading into the gallery and great ftairs, relieves all the other apartments : this ferves alfo for a room of general rendezvous, and for public entertainments, with illuminations, dancing, and mufic. The form is new and fingular; it is a circle within a circle, the fmaller opening into a larger, by eight peircings, adorned with columns, and terminated with niches and ftatues, fo that the fcenery, like the decorations of a theatre, apparently increafes the extent, and leaves room for the imagination to play.

The private apartments are now the only part of the plan remaining undefcribed; on one hand is the Dutchefs's bed-chamber, an antiroom for the attendance of her maids, her toilet or dreffing-room, her powdering-room, water-clofet, and outer anti-room, with a back ftair leading to interfols for the maids bed-room and wardrobes, &c. On the other hand is a dreffing-room for the Duke, a powdering-room, writing-room, water-clofet and ftairs to interfols for His Grace's valet-de-chambre, and wardrobe, &c. In thefe, little form is neceffary, and none is here attempted, except what may ferve in fome meafure to diverfity the fcene.

We fhould not have dared to enter fo minutely into the defcription of this plan, if we did not imagine that this is one of thofe branches of our art, which has not hitherto been treated of with any accuracy, or ftudied with any care; though of all others the moft effential, both to the fplendor and convenience of life.

PLATE VI.

Section of the two ends of the HALL *fhowing the fquare and femicircular receffes, as alfo the fteps, rifing to the anti-room, and the additional fcenery occafioned by that circumftance.*

PLATE VII.

Detail, or parts of the HALL *at large.*

The vafe is allowed to have a fine effect in execution, as have alfo the trophies and other parts of the decoration, which are in a great, but fimple ftyle, fuitable to the fubject.

The whole is in ftucco, admirably executed by Mr. Rofe.

PLATE VIII.

Mifcellaneous defigns of various pieces of FURNITURE, *done for different perfons, which are here introduced in order to give more utility and diverfity to the work, and contains as follows :*

Defigns of a glafs-frame and commode-table; upon which is placed a clock and vafes, with branches for candles. Thefe were executed for us in wood gilt, except the vafes which are of filver.

To the right is a bracket and vafe, with branches for candles, executed in wood for James Bourdieu, Efq.

To the left is alfo a bracket and vafe, with branches for candles, executed in wood gilt, for George Keate, Efq.

To the right is a tripod, defigned for the Earl of Coventry, with a vafe for candles.

To the left is another tripod, defigned for the Earl of Coventry, with a vafe and branches for three candles, executed in or moulu, for Sir Laurence Dundafs, and afterwards for the Duke of Bolton.

II
PREFACE.

VARIOUS avocations have retarded the publifhing of our fecond number longer than we intended. During this interval, we have liftened with refpect to the opinion of the public concerning the firft number; and we have had the moft flattering approbation from men of tafte, both at home and abroad.

Encouraged by this, we now refume our tafk, with greater confidence, by publifhing the plans, elevations, and fections of Kenwood; a beautiful villa belonging to Lord Mansfield, the friend of every elegant art and ufeful fcience.

We have referved the remaining defigns of Sion for

fome future number; as we were perfuaded, that by giving fpecimens of fome of our other works, we fhould add greater variety to our undertaking, without diminifhing its utility. — As in this work we aim, not only at affording entertainment to the connoiffeur, but wifh alfo to convey fome inftruction to the artift; we fhall, from time to time, make fuch obfervations as naturally arife from the subjects before us. — Should we differ in any of thefe obfervations from the opinion of either antient or modern authors, we do not mean to engage in any controverfy, being only defirous of fubmitting our ideas to the confideration of the public. At the fame time we may affirm, that whatever we venture either to publifh, or to recommend, is the refult of much experience, and of a careful fearch into the pureft fources of antiquity. — Architecture has not, like fome others arts, an immediate ftandard in nature, to which the artift can always refer, and which would enable the fkilful inftlantly to decide with refpectt to the degree of excellence attained in any work. In architecture, it muft be formed and improved by a correct tafte, and diligent ftudy of the beauties exhibited by great mafters in their productions; and it is only by profound meditation upon thefe, that one becomes capable of diftinguifhing between what is graceful and what is inelegant; between that which poffeffes, and that which is deftitute of harmony.

We have obferved in our firft number, that many of the difputes among modern architects are extremely frivolous. There is nothing with refpect to which they have differed more, than their rules for the diminution of columns. This, however, is a fubject of greater importance than those which frequently engage their attention. The column is not only one of the nobleft and moft graceful pieces of decoration, but in all round bodies, efpecially fuch as ftand infulated, there is a delicacy of proportion to be obferved, that thofe of another form, and in other fituations, do not require. Without entering into any critical difquifitions concerning the opinions of either the antients or moderns with refpect to this point, we fhall only obferve, that our conftant practice has been, to diminifh our columns from the bafe to the capital, by means of the inftrument ufed by Nicomedes for defcribing the firft conchoid, wich we think has exceeded in elegance any other method hitherto employed. But as this inftrument and the manner of ufing it, has already been explained by fome modern authors, we fhould not here have ventured to mention it, had it not been to recommend it, as preferable to all others.

The proportion of columns has alfo been a fubject of much enquiry. But as this greatly depends upon the fituation of thefe columns, whether they make parts of outfide, or infide decoration, whether they ftand infulated, or engaged, whether raifed much above the eye, or level with it; thefe are circumftances which very much affect fuch proportions, and confequently leave an uncertainty, which can only be properly afcertained by the correct tafte of the fkilful and experienced artift.

Having mentioned the diminution and proportion of columns, we are naturally led to. make fome obfervations with regard to their capitals; an object of great diftinction and delicacy in the detail of architecture. — In the firft place, we acknowledge only three orders; the Doric, the Ionic, and the Corinthian: for as to the Tufcan, it is, in fact, no more than a bad and imperfect Doric; and the Compofite, or Roman order, in our opinion, is a very difagreable and awkward mixture of the Corinthian and Ionic, without either grace or beauty. We do not however mean to condemn the compofing of capitals; a liberty which has been often taken by the antients with great fuccefs; and in a former part of this work, we have exhibited an attempt of our own in this way; and fhall, during the courfe of it, have other opportunities of the fame kind.

The Doric capital, when properly adorned, is capable of great elegance : But where rich decoration is required, in order to give it all it's grace, the neck, or fpace between the aftragal and the annulets, fhould be made of much greater height than the common proportion prefcribed by Paladio and many other moderns; and that neck fhould be enriched in the various ways which we fhall have occafion to reprefent in the courfe of our work. — One example of this kind is to be feen in the capital of the Pilafters to the fouth front, given at large in the fourth plate.

The Corinthian capital itfelf does not, in our opinion, admit of more dignity and magnificence, than a rich Ionic with it's volutes fquare in the front. — Angular volutes, as in the Temples of Concord and Manly Fortune at Rome, and in the Temple of Erectheus at Athens, have always appeared to us lefs folid, lefs grave, and lefs graceful; and, in our opinion, they have been injudicioufly adopted by Michael Angelo, Scamozzi, and many other modern architects. Their reafon for this was, in order to avoid the irregularity of appearance in this capital when viewed in profile which differs fo very much from it's afpect in front. But notwithftanding this difference, the profile itfelf, as well as the front, are fufceptible of fuch beauties, that we are inclinable to hazard fome defects, rather than to facrifice the elegant refult of the whole compofition.

There may indeed be fome cafes, where fuch irregularity in the capital might be attended with great inconvenience, as in a fquare or oblong building furrounded by this order: But in this, or fimilar cafes, it would be much more eligible for the fkilful architect to fubftitute another order in it's place.

The great fize of the volute of the Grecian Ionic has always appeared to us by much too heavy, and thofe ufed by the Romans feem rather to border on the other extreme. We have therefore generally taken a mean between them, which we think has a happy effect; making them in width about one half of the fuperior diameter of the column, and obferving that the center of the eye of the volute is nearly perpendicular to the extremity of the faid diameter.

We have alfo adopted the Grecian manner of forming the volute with a double fillet, which, by producing more light and fhade, gives great relief, and far exceeds in grace and beauty that ufed by the Romans. In imitation of the Greeks, we likewife bend the channel, or hollow band, from whence the volutes fpring, in the middle of the capital; which band, in cafe of rich decoration, fhould be filled with a winding foliage; or fome fuch ornament, from the center of the capital to the eye of the volute. But the members of chief importance towards compleating this capital, are the aftragal and neck, which neck, as in the Doric, fhould be filled fometimes with various enrichments, more or lefs ornamented, and fometimes, perhaps, fhould be left altogether plain, according to the ftile of the building where it is employed. In the example exhibited in this number, this capital has the addition of a plain neck and fillet, without which it always appears flat and meagre. In a future number, we fhall have occasion to give an example of it, executed at Sion-Houfe, with all the embellifhment of which it is capable.

The foliage and ftems of the Corinthian capital make it not only magnificent, but alfo extremely gay and graceful. It has befides fome advantages over the Ionic in point of form; all it's fides are regular, and the concavity of it's abacus contrafts in a beautiful manner with the convexity of the vafe. The form of the vafe is fometimes executed in a moft defective manner, by fwelling it towards the middle, and bending it inwards at the bottom, in a cimarecta fhape; which is both unpleafant, and refts ill upon the fhaft of the column. — This error has probably been introduced from a defect in the drawing of the plates of Defgodetz, whom, notwithftanding his great parade of precifion and accuracy, we have often found guilty of confiderable overfights and miftakes, not only in his menfuration, but alfo in the delineation of many of the antient monuments. This capital, as well as the preceeding, we think may be formed into various compofitions, of great beauty and elegance, as we fhall endeavour to fhew by fome examples hereafter.

We fhall not at prefent enter into any particular detail with refpect to the entablatures or the bafes of the different orders, but refer to the fpecimens of each now publifhed, and to what we are about to publifh. We muft however beg leave to obferve, that we can fee no reafon for affigning to each order it's precife entablature, fixed down unalterably both in figure and dimenfion. Different circumftances of fituation and propriety ought to vary the form, and alfo the proportion, of all entablatures. A latitude in this refpect, under the and of an ingenious and able artift, is often productive of great novelty, variety and beauty.

The reader has before him in this number two compofitions of this kind, the one Doric, the other Ionic, neither of which are fubjected to any precife rule, and yet the refult of the whole has always been deemed very pleafing.

The mouldings in the remaining ftructures of antient Rome are confiderably lefs curvelineal than thofe of the antient monuments of Greece. We have always given a preference to the latter, and have even thought it advifeable to bend them ftill more in many cafes, particularly in interior finifhings, where objects are near, and ought to be foftened to the eye; for circular mouldings are intended to relieve the fight from the acutenefs of the fquare ones, of which too frequent a repetition would be infinitely harfh and tirefome: But in bending the cimarecta, the cimareverfa or talon, the ovolo, the cavetto, and the aftragal, in the method we have always followed, as may be feen from our defigns, they blend and mingle themfelves more harmonioufly with the ſquare members, and attain more delicacy and elegance, than ſuch as have been commonly uſed.

PLANS, ELEVATIONS, and SECTIONS of KENWOOD,

AFTER THE

DESIGNS of ROBERT ADAM.

WHATEVER defeƈts, either in beauty or compoſition, ſhall be discovered in the following deſigns, they muſt be imputed to me alone; for the noble proprietor, with his uſual liberality of ſentiment, gave full ſcope to my ideas: nor were theſe confined by any circumſtances, but the neceſſity of preſerving the proper exterior ſimilitude between the new and the old parts of the building; and even with reſpeƈt to this, where the latter appeared defeƈtive in it's detail, I was at full liberty to make the proper deviations; the parts of which are repreſented at large in the fourth plate.

EXPLANATION of the PLATES.

PLATE I.

Plan of KENWOOD,

Of which the portico to the north, the great room or library, and its anti-room, are the new additions. But as many alterations were made, and many inſide decorations added, in the apartments of the old houſe, theſe are reſerved as the ſubjeƈt of another number.

The great room, with its anti-room, was begun by Lord Mansfield's orders, in the year 1767, and was intended both for a library and a room for receiving company. The circular receſſes were therefore fitted up for the former purpoſe, and the ſquare part, or body of the room, was made ſuitable to the latter. The whole is reckoned elegant in it's proportions and decorations, and the cieling in particular, which is a ſegment of a circle, has been generally admired.

PLATE II.

View of the south Front of KENWOOD, *with the* TERRACE *and* RISING BANK.

A great body of water covers the bottom, and ſerves to go round a large natural wood of tall trees riſing one above another upon the ſides of a hill. Over the vale, through which the water flows, there is a noble view let into the houſe and terrace, of the city of London, Greenwich Hoſpital, the River Thames, the ſhips paſſing up and down, with an extenſive proſpeƈt, but clear and diſtinƈt, on both ſides of the river. To the north-eaſt, and weſt of the houſe and terrace, the mountainous villages of Highgate and Hampſtead form delightful objeƈts. The whole ſcene is amazingly gay, magnificent, beautiful, and piƈtureſque. The hill and dale are finely diverſified; nor is it eaſy to imagine a ſituation more ſtriking without, or more agreeably retired and peaceful within.

The decoration beſtowed on this front of the houſe is suitable to such a ſcene. The idea is new, and has been generally approved.

PLATE III.

Geometrical Elevations of the ſouth and north Fronts of KENWOOD.

The portico to the north is the only part of that front which is new. The decoration of the south front, excepting that of the weſt wing, is entirely new, and became in ſome meaſure neceſſary, to conceal the brick-work, which being built at different times, was of various colours. — The Attic ſtory is a late addition to the houſe, and was executed in a ſingular manner, the walls being raiſed, and the new roof covered in, before the old one was removed; and thus was the houſe left habitable, and unexpoſed to the injuries of the weather, during the whole progreſs of this uſeful alteration.

PLATE IV.

Detail, or parts at large of the ſouth Front.

PLATE V.

Section of one of the Sides of the great Room.

The ſquare receſſes on this ſide are fitted up with glaſſes, which, refleƈting the objeƈts that are ſeen from windows, have a moſt ſingular and beautiful effeƈt.

PLATE VI.

Section of one End of the great Room;

Which ſhews the ſcreen of columns that ſeparates the body, or middle part of the room, from the circular receſſes, the receſſes themſelves, with the manner of finiſhing the book-caſes. The freeſe, over the columns, is enriched with an ornament compoſed of lions and the heads of deer; the former being the ſupporters, and the latter the creſt of the family. In this plate is alſo the deſign of the chimney piece, at large, elegantly executed in ſtatuary marble.

PLATE VII.

The Cieling of the great Room,

Which is in the form and ſtyle of thoſe of the ancients. It is an imitation of a flat arch, which is extremely beautiful, and much more perfeƈt than that which is commonly called the coved cieling, when there is height ſufficient to admit of it, as in the preſent caſe. The coved cieling, which is a portion or quadrant of a circle around the room, and riſing to a flat in the center, ſeems to be altogether of modern invention, and admits of ſome elegance in the decoration. It is a ſort of middle way, between the flat or horizontal cieling, and the various forms of arched ones praƈtiſed by the ancients. As it does not require ſo much height as the latter mode, it has been found of great uſe in the finiſhing of modern apartments; but, neither is it's form ſo grand, nor does it admit of ſo much beauty of decoration, as the ancient arched cielings; which conſiſt of three kinds, the dome, the groin, and the plain trunk arch, ſuch as that now before us, with their various combinations.

All the cielings of the ancients, which continue ſtill to be the objeƈts of admiration, not only on account of their beauty, but alſo of their duration, were executed in one or other of theſe modes.

In the courfe of this work, there will be occafion to give feveral examples of each kind, as they have been executed after my own and my brother's defigns.

The ftucco work of this cieling, and of the other decorations, is finely executed, by Mr. Jofeph Rofe. The paintings are elegantly performed, by Mr. Antonio Zucchi, a Venetian painter, of great eminence; and the grounds of the pannels and freefes are coloured with light tints of pink and green, fo as to take off the glare of white, fo common in every cieling, till of late. This always appeared to me fo cold and unfinifhed, that I ventured to introduce this variety of grounds, at once to relieve the ornaments, remove the crudenefs of the white, and create a harmony between the cieling and the fidewals, with their hangings, pictures, and other decorations.

It is with much pleafure that I find my own ideas concerning the effect which this would produce, juftified by experience, and confirmed by the opinion of every perfon who has feen this room: But what is ftill more agreeable to me, is the entire fatisfaction which it has always given to the noble proprietor himfelf.

PLATE VIII.

Designs of various Pieces of Furniture done for this Villa;

Which are here introduced, in order to give more utility and diverfity to the work.

III
P R E F A C E.

WE proceed to lay before the public another number of our Works. It contains a part of the defigns of LUTON HOUSE, one of the feats of the EARL OF BUTE. We are happy in having this opportunity of expreffing to the world that gratitude which we never ceafed to feel, for the protection, favour, and friendfhip with which we have always been honoured by his Lordfhip.

After having made various defigns for Luton Houfe in different ftyles, the Earl of Bute fixed upon the following, and directed it to be carried into execution. In confequence of his Lordfhip's orders, the work was begun in 1767; and whatever reputation the Architect may acquire at prefent by this plan, that which moft flatters his vanity, and will do him the greateft honour with pofterity, is the approbation of the noble proprietor, fo juftly efteemed for his great tafte and difcerning judgment in the celebrated works of the ancients, and in every branch of the fine arts.

The fituation of the Houfe is peculiarly fortunate. It ftands on the eafy declivity of a hill or bank; at the bottom of which, along the vale, runs the river Lee, a clear and beautiful ftream, fpreading into an artificial lake, upwards of a mile and a half in length, and in fome places of great breadth, as it covers a fpace of near fifty acres.

The bank on which the Houfe is built, as well as the rifing grounds on the oppofite fide of the lake, are beautifully diverfified by gentle rifings and fallings; and the whole park is adorned with lofty foreft trees of different kinds, happilly difpofed, fo as to create variety in the views, and produce a ftriking effect in the landfcape.

The Houfe itfelf, which is built of a bright coloured ftone, of a bluifh caft, and admirably wrought, adds greatly to the magnificence and fplendor of a scene univerfally admired.

E X P L A N A T I O N   O F   T H E   P L A T E S.

PLATE I.

Plan of Luton Houfe as originally designed.

PLATE II.

Plan of Luton Houfe with alterations.

In that part already executed, the library makes a very noble and extenfive apartment.

PLATE III.

Elevation of the principal or weft Front of Luton Houfe.

The alterations of the plan, from what was originally intented, have produced a fingular effect upon this front, in which, there being no apartments, and confequently no windows required except in the bows towards each end, that circumftance has permitted the introducing a kind of exterior decoration, which refembles that of a publick work rather than of a private building, and gives an air of dignity and grandeur, of which few dwelling-houfes are fufceptible.

PLATE IV.

Elevation of the east front of Luton Houfe towards the river.

PLATE V.

Elevation of the north and south fronts of Luton Houfe :

In the latter of which there is a degree of light and fhade, which gives it a peculiarly good effect in the execution.

PLATE VI.

Detail, or parts at large of the Saloon and great Stairs.

The capital of the order in the faloon is altered from an antique one, the drawing of which his Lordfhip brought from abroad, and is an example of the latitude which the ancients often took in compofitions of this kind. A fimilar latitude is taken with regard to the compofition of the cornice, which is not fubjected to any of the cuftomary rules : yet we have the fatisfaction to find it has been approved of by men of tafte.

The capital to the fcreen of columns in the great ftairs is alfo new. These having been very clofely imitated in various places, particularly in the Pantheon in Oxford Street, fhew the approbation they have met with from the public.

It does not appear neceffary to mention the reft of the detail in this plate, which will not be found altogether of the common kind hitherto ufed.

PLATE VII.

Ceiling of Lady Bute's dreffing Room, which is coved.

The flat part is richly decorated with ftucco ornaments, by Mr. Rofe, and paintaings by Mr. Zucchi. The grounds are alfo coloured with various tints to take off the crudenefs of the white.

PLATE VIII.

Defigns of different pieces of furniture done for this Houfe.

The ftove-grate defigned and executed for his Lordfhip in the year 1768, as it was the firft decorated in this manner, feems to have given the idea of thofe in this form which now prevail so much both in public and private buildings.

The cornices for window-curtains, with a great variety of other designs for this purpofe, which we fhall have occafion to give hereafter, were intended as an attempt to banifh the abfurd French compofitions of this kind, heretofore fo fervilely imitated by the upholfterers of this country.

The brafs candelabra which ftand in the niches of the drawing room were brought from abroad by the Earl of Bute, and are in the ftyle of modern Italy. They are evidently the compofition of fome painter or ftatuary who has facrificed the fimple and the graceful to the bufy and the picturefque. Somewhat of this ftile has been imitated in the pedeftals on which they ftand, that there might appear a degree of harmony through the whole.

IV
PREFACE.

PUBLIC Buildings are the moft fplendid monuments of a great and opulent people. The purpofes for which they are intended, admit of magnificence in the defign, and require folidity in the conftruction.

Such buildings muft, of courfe, contain great and fpacious apartments for the meeting of numerous affemblies; and, confequently, they are fufceptible of more grandeur, as well in their external decoration, as in their internal diftribution.

The frequent, but neceffary, repetition of windows in private houfes, cuts the façade into minute parts, which render it difficult, if not impoffible, to preferve that greatnefs and fimplicity of compofition, which, by impofing on the imagination, ftrikes the mind.

The mafter, who has not an opportunity to diftinguifh himfelf by difplaying his abilities in works of real greatnefs, will naturally betake himfelf to other refources, and, following the moft approved examples of Greece and Rome, endeavour to call forth the admiration of mankind by the beauty and variety of his forms, by the richnefs and fertility of his invention, and by the elegance and delicacy of his ornamental decorations. All thefe may be adopted with great propriety in fmall rooms and private appartments.

In this refpect, painting and architecture may very juftly be compared. The moft celebrated painters of the Italian fcholl, trufting to the greatnefs of their compofitions, to their large maffes of light and fhade, and to the fplendor and eclat of their general effect, never entered with fcrupulous minutenefs into all the detail of the various parts; whilft the Flemifh artift, fenfible of the fmallnefs of his field, endeavours to avail himfelf of every particular circumftance, by entering with precision into the confideration of the minute detail, by defcribing every part with the utmoft accuracy and correctnefs, and by heightening with force and brilliancy of colour every acceffary that can give elegance and vivacity to his fmall, but exquifite ond highly finifhed, performance.

Horace complains, that, in his time, the Romans were become extremely expenfive in their private houfes and gardens; which circumftance rendered them lefs capable of expending large fums upon, and of attending to, the decoration and magnificence of their public buildings. Our anceftors, fays he, were exceedingly economical with regard to themfelves and their private houfes, but profufe and magnificent in whatever concerned the public edifices, particularly thofe which related to the fervice of the Gods*.

The bigoted zeal and fuperftitious pomp of the Roman-Catholic religion have produced a like profufion and magnificence in the public works of modern Italy; and to that caufe, however incompatible it may feem to be with general fcience and liberal ideas, Italy owes it's vaft progrefs and prefent fplendor in the arts of elegance.

Great-Britain, fince the firft acquired power and opulence, has never had the fame motive for calling forth abilities and talents or the fine arts : neither has the form of our government, nor the decent fimplicity of our religion, ever demanded any fuch exertion; nor is it probable that they ever will while we continue a free and flourifhing people. Though, therefore, we have, within a fhort period of years, made confiderable progrefs in almoft every art; and demonftrated, by many convincing proofs, that this country, when roufed, is capable of admirable efforts of native genius; yet we muft not expect that the fine arts will ever meet with their moft ample reward, or attain their utmoft degree of perfection, deprived as they are of that emulation which is excited by public works, and by the honourable applaufe of a refined and difcerning Public.

---

* Jam pauca aratro jugera regiæ
Moles relinquent : undique latius
Extenta vifentur Lucrino
Stagna Lacu.

And afterwards :

Privatus illis cenfus erat brevis,
Commune magnum : nulla decempedis
Metata privatis opacam
Porticus excipiebat Arcton :
Nec fortuitum fpernere cefpitem
Leges finebant, oppida publico
Sumptu jubentes, & deorum
Templa novo decorare faxo. LIB. II. CARMEN 15.

We cannot help thinking that there is fomewhat very fingular in this obfervation of Horace. At the time in which the poet wrote, there were certainly greater public works erected and reftored at Rome, than ever had been in any former period.

Suetonius, in the Life of Auguftus, fays, " Principes viros hortatus eft, ut pro facultate " quifque monumentis vel novis, vel refectis, et excultis urbem adornaret. Multa itaque " opera à multis extructa funt. "

We fhall here mention fome of the principal buildings erected in the reign of Auguftus, and, for a more particular account of them, refer our readers to the " Campus Martius " of Piranezi, where they will find quoted every ancient authority on this fubject.

In the year of Rome 720 was erected the Curia, the Schools, a noble Portico, which furrounded the Temple of Jupiter and Juno, with a Library adjoining.

In 723, Statilius Taurus finifhed an Amphitheatre built at his own expence.

In 724, the Temple of Minerva, called the Chalcidica, was built of brafs.

In 725, Auguftus built a moft magnificent Maufoleum for himfelf and family.

In 726, Agrippa erected the Pantheon, which ftill remains entire.

In 727, Agrippa dedicated the Septa, for containing the Comitia Tributa.

In 728, he erected the Portico of Neptune, and adjoining thereto built the Temple and Bafilica of that Deity. He added to the Pantheon the noble Portico which now remains, and likewife built the Thermae behind the Pantheon, for the exercife of the body according to the Lacedemonian manner. Of this immenfe building we have a plan ingenioufly imagined by Pyranezi, from the defcription of ancient authors; and we have alfo one preferved by Palladio, taken from the remains which were to be feen in his time. This is now in our poffeffion, but never was publifhed.

In 730, Agrippa built the Theatre of Marcellus, of there which ftill are great remains; and another Theatre was erected much about the fame time by Cornelius Balbus.

In 734, Agrippa brought the Aqua Virginis into Rome by an Aqueduct of upwards of fourteen miles in length.

Befides the Aqua Virginis, he had diftributed through the Campus Martius a great part of the water of the ancient Anienis and the Marcia, repaired their conduits, and beautified the city with many Fountains; making alfo the neceffary Sewers for carrying the fuperfluity into the Tiber.

In 743, Auguftus prefented to the Sun the great Obelifk of Sefoftris brought by him to Rome, and erected it as the gnomon to a Sun-dial.

In 746, Auguftus gave to the people of Rome the field of Agrippa, and the Diribitorium, a building begun by Agrippa for paying the army and diftributing donatives to the people.

Paula, fifter to Agrippa, alfo began a Portico, which she left unfinifhed.

There were likewife erected in this reign the Portico of the Nations, that of Europe, that of Philip, and many other edifices of lefs confequence, which we fhall not enumerate; having already tranfgreffed much by the length of this Note.

We fhall only farther obferve, that, from this formidable lift, we think, we have clearly proved, that, notwithftanding the above-quoted lines of Horace, it was not poffible the grandeur and decoration of public works could be neglected at a time when the ingenious Vitruvius lived, and the fplendid Auguftus reigned.

EXPLANATION of the PLATES.

PLATE I.

View of part of Whitehall, fhewing the Screen of Colums in front of the Admiralty.

Which forms the gateway to that building, with a porter's lodge and other offices at each end. The whole is compofed of a fimple Doric, to correspond, in fome degree, with the extreme plainnefs ot the building within. The gateway and pavilions adjoining to the fouth end of the fcreen were alfo defigned and executed by Robert Adam, as an entry for the Earl of Kinnoul, then proprietor of that houfe.

PLATE II.

Elevation of the Board-Room for the Paymafter general and the other Commiffioners of Chelfea-Hofpital, with an office for Invalids, &c.

This building, which is fituated nearly oppofite to the Admiralty, being almoft in a ruinous condition, Robert Adam was ordered, by the Right Honble. Richard Rigby, the prefent Paymafter-general, and the Board, to put it in repair, and to beftow fome decorations on the front towards Whitehall; one of the moft public ftreets in London, leading from almoft every quarter of the town to the courts of juftice and houfes of parliament.

PLATE III.

Plan of the Houfe of the Society of Arts, Manufactures, and Commerce; with a Houfe adjoining for their Secretary.

PLATE IV.

Elevation of the Houfe of the Society of Arts, Manufactures and Commerce.

Situated on the north fide of John Street, in the Adelphi.

PLATE V.

Plan of two stories of a Regifter-office or Houfe for containing the Records of Scotland,

Situated in the new town of Edinburgh, facing the bridge. This building, fo much wanted and fo exceedingly neceffary for the prefervation of the public records of that country, was begun in June 1774, and the fondation ftone was laid by the Right Honourable Lord Frederick Campbell, the prefent Lord-regifter for Scotland, and the other principal officers of ftate there, as truftees. Upon that ftone was the following infcription :

CONSERVANDIS TABULIS PUBLICIS
POSITUM EST
MUNIFICENTIA OPTIMI ET PIENTISSIMI REGIS
GEORGII TERTII,
ANNO MDCCLXXIV.

The various offices which this building contains, being extremely numerous, are marked, and their ufes explained, upon the margin of the plans.

PLATE VI.

Elevation of the Regifter-Office,

Fronting fouth, on the bridge, of communication between the old and new town of Edinburgh.

PLATE VII.

Section of the Regifter-Office from South to North,

Shewing the great circular faloon, which ferves as an additional repofitory for records, and at the fame time furnifhes acceffes to many of the apartments on both ftories of the building. This fection alfo fhews the ends of the porter's hall and writers hall on the ground ftory; and the ends of the lord-regifter's and truftees room, and the room for the infpecting and extracting of writs, on the firft floor.

PLATE VIII.

Various Pieces of ornamental furniture.

Which have been defigned and executed for different perfons.

V

PREFACE.

WHOEVER attempts to trace the progrefs of nations in fcience or in tafte, will meet with fingular appearances, of which it is not eafy to give any account. In Italy, national genius awakened at once, and exerted itfelf with vigour, in every direction. The fixteenth century is the fplendid age of that country; and during the courfe of it, flourifhed the great poets, hiftorians, painters, fculptors, architects, and muficians, whom the Italians ftill confider as the models of perfect compofition, and follow as their mafters and guides. In England, the firft efforts of national genius, though more circumfcribed, were not lefs vigorous. This country can boaft of poffeffing a great dramatic poet, long before any nation on the north fide of the Alps had produced an author worthy of that name. The exertions of England in the culture of fcience have been ftill greater, and more meritorious. Bacon early pointed out the path by which genuine philofophy fhould advance to the difcovery of truth. By adhering to it, Newton penetrated into the fecrets of nature, and explained its laws. Locke traced and developed the operations of the human mind.

But whilft England led the way in thofe important inveftigations, fhe could not boaft of the fame pre-eminence in the fine arts. In painting, fculpture, architecture, and mufic, her progrefs was extremely flow; and in all of them fhe has been far excelled by other nations of modern Europe.

If, however, we were to diftinguifh any one of thefe arts as more cultivated and more fuccefsful in England, we fhould not hefitate to fay it was Architecture. Inigo Jones, who had long ftudied in Italy, rescued this art in a confiderable degree from the Gothicifm of former times, and began to introduce into his country a love of that elegance and refinement which characterife the productions of Greece and Rome.

Inftructed and encouraged by his example, Sir Chriftopher Wren became more chafte; and having the felicity to be employed in executing the moft magnificent work of Englifh architecture, he was enabled to difplay greater extent of genius.

Vanburgh underftood better than either the art of living among the great. A commodious arrangement of apartments was therefore his peculiar merit. But his lively imagination fcorned the reftraint of any rule in compofition; and his paffion for what was fancifully magnificent, prevented him from difcerning what was truly fimple, elegant, and fublime.

Campbell, Gibbs, and Kent, have each their peculiar fhare of merit.

But whilft England was thus adorned with a fucceffion of confiderable mafters in architecture, the various departments of painting, as well as of the kindred arts connected with it, have been almoft wholly engroffed by foreigners. It is by the pencils of ftrangers that the lineaments of the heroes, ftatefmen, and beauties, of former times are known to their defcendants.

The progrefs of all thefe arts in Great Britain may be confidered as the peculiar diftinction of the prefent reign. Inferior to our anceftors in fcience, we furpafs them in tafte. The ftudy of what is elegant and beautiful, fenfibility, difcernment, and a correctnefs of eye, are become more general; and arts formerly little known begin to be naturalized amongft us. Cherifhed by the patronage of a people, opulent, difcerning, and capable of eftimating merit, the genius of native artifts has been called forth into new and laudable exertions. Many of the inferior branches dependant on painting, architecture, and fculpture, have been carried, within that fhort period, to a degree of perfection which has far exceeded the efforts of artifts in any other part of modern Europe.

A Britifh fchool of painting may be gradually formed, and vie for eminence with thofe of other nations. Architecture has already become more elegant and more interefting. The parade, the convenience, and focial pleafures of life, being better underftood, are more ftrictly attended to in the arrangement and difpofition of apartments. Greater variety of form, greater beauty in defign, greater gaiety and elegance of ornament, are introduced into interior decoration; while the outfide compofition is more fimple, more grand, more varied in its contour, and impofes on the mind from the fuperior magnitude and movement of its parts.

Without detracting from the talents and merit of other artifts, we are encouraged, by the public approbation, to flatter ourfelves, that our works have fomewhat contributed to diffufe jufter ideas and a better tafte in architecture. It was with a view of rendering them more generally ufeful, that we firft engaged in this publication.

This Number, which is the laft of the Firft Volume, contains fome of our defigns for the King, the Queen, and her Royal Highnefs the late Princefs Dowager of

Wales. Tho thefe we have fubjoined the defign of a magnificent harpficord, executed here for the Emprefs of Ruffia.

EXPLANATION of the PLATES.

PLATE I.

Defign of a Gateway for Carleton Houfe in Pall-Mall, done for her Royal Highnefs the late Princefs Dowager of Wales.

As the prefent court wall to Carleton Houfe is extremely mean and irregular, her Royal Highnefs was defirous of remedying thofe defects, in fuch a manner as might render the approach to her town refidence more proper and elegant. With this view the following defign was formed, and confiderable alterations were likewife propofed to be made upon the plan of the houfe itfelf : all of which were fo much approved of by her Royal Highnefs, that fhe had determined to have carried them into execution, if the declining ftate of her health had not prevented any fteps from being taken towards the completion of this favourite plan.

The center part of this building is in the ftyle of a triumphal arch. On each fide is a range of ornamented pilafters, with niches between them intended for ftatues reprefenting a feries of the fovereigns of Great Britain. Over the columns and pilafters are placed trophies, meant to commemorate the victories at the clofe of the laft and commencement of the prefent reign. These were not only introduced as fuitable ornaments for fuch a building, but alfo in order to prevent the repetition of ftatues, which appear meagre in fuch fituations. The Britifh arms fill the pannels over the doors of the middle part.

This Plate contains likewife the plan of the gateway, with the colonade propofed towards the court, which would have formed a noble decoration to that fide, and at the fame time would have afforded convenient fhelter to attendants. The boxes for the fentinels are practifed in the piers of the gates.

PLATE II.

Defign at large of the Entablature and Britannic Order.

We have formerly mentioned, that the ancients ufed very frequently to indulge themfelves in compofitions of fancy; introducing into their capitals and entablatures the various fymbols of thofe divinities to whom they erected temples. A licence of the fame kind haf been hazarded here. The lion and unicorn fupport the angles of the abacus, which is adorned with the regal crown, the collar of the order of the Garter, and acorns in the ovolo. The fceptre and dove, the rofe and thiftle, fill the intermediate fpace between the leaves of the acanthus. The lion and unicorn are alfo alternately interwoven in the foliage of the freeze, and the oak-leaf and acorn again adorn the upper torus of the bafe.

PLATE III.

This Plate contains feveral of the parts at large, viz.

The pannels over the doors of the center gateway.

One of the trophies over the pediments of the end gateways.

One of the trophies over the pilafters, and the pateras in the fpaundrels of the arches.

PLATE IV.

Two defigns of Chimnies :

One of which is executed in the great faloon of the Queen's Houfe, and the other propofed for a room in the palace of St. James's.

In the freeze of the former, the crown and fupporters are introduced as part of the ornament, and on the tablet of the latter is a bas-relief of the Aldobrandini marriage.

PLATE V.

Original Defign of an Illumination and Tranfparency, part of which was executed, by command of the Queen, in June 1762, in honour of his Majefty's birth-day.

PLATE VI.

Defign of a Sedan-Chair, executed for the Queen.

PLATE VII.

Defign of a painted Cieling, executed in the room called the Japanned Room, in the Queen's Houfe.

PLATE VIII.

Defign of a Harpfichord, inlaid with various-coloured woods, executed in London for the Emprefs of Ruffia.

This defign was confiderably altered by the perfon who executed the work.

THE

WORKS IN ARCHITECTURE

OF

ROBERT AND JAMES ADAM, ESQUIRES.

VOLUME II.

Containing the Five following NUMBERS, viz.

I. The HOUSE of the EARL of DERBY, in GROSVENOR-SQUARE.
II. The HOUSE of SIR WATKIN WILLIAMS WYNN, BARONET, in ST. JAMES'S-SQUARE
III. The HOUSE of the EARL of SHELBURNE, in BERKELEY-SQUARE.
IV. The SEAT of the DUKE of NORTHUMBERLAND, at SION, continued.
V. Various DESIGNS of PUBLIC and PRIVATE BUILDINGS.

LONDON: Printed for the AUTHORS;
And fold by PETER ELMSLY, oppofite Southampton-Street, in the Strand, and by the other Bookfellers in Town and Country.
MDCCLXXIX.

PREFACE.

FROM this Number, persons of taste will, no doubt, observe, that a mode of Decoration has been here attempted, which differs from any thing hitherto ractised in Europe: for, although the style of the ornament, and the colouring of the Countess of DERBY's dressing-room, are both evidently imitated from the vases and urns of the Etruscans, yet we have not been able to discover, either in our researches into antiquity, or in the works of modern artists, any idea of applying this taste to the decoration of apartments (A.).

When we consider this fact with attention, we cannot help thinking it extremely singular. There is surely nothing better ascertained from historical authority, than that the Romans borrowed, not only many of their customs, their civil institutions, and religious ceremonies, but also their first knowledge of every art and science, from their ancient and ingenious neighbours, the Etruscans (B.).

Long before their acquaintance with the Greeks, the Romans had derived from Etruria such information as enabled them to make a very considerable progress in many branches of architecture (C.). This accounts for the great and masterly style in which they planned and constructed their public works from the most early period (D.).

We learn too, from good authority, that this elegant manufacture of earthenware was early established among the Etruscans, particularly in the city of Aretium, now Arezzo (E.).

That the Romans must have been well acquainted with this taste during the whole course of their greatness is almost certain, from the vast number of beautiful vases and urns which have been found in every part of Italy within these three centuries, and which now adorn both the public collections and the private cabinets of the curious all over Europe (F.). It is nevertheless remarkable, that neither in

Adrian's villa, where so much attention was paid to elegance and variety, nor in the Cryptæ of Rome or of Baia, nor in any part of Herculaneum or Pompeia, has any fragment been yet produced of interior decoration, executed in the taste now before us.

We have mentioned these circumstances, with more particular attention, in order that, if judges in architecture shall think any praise due to the discovery of another class of decoration and embellishment, they may know to whom the art is indebted for this improvement.

The noble proprietor of this magnificent residence has not, however, been long the sole possessor of this new style of decoration. Many persons of rank and fortune having been struck and pleased with the taste, several apartments of the same kind were immediately designed, and have been executed under our direction at the house of Earl Bathurst, and that of the Countess Dowager of Home in Town, and at Mr. Child's, at Osterley Park, in the County of Middlesex.

(A) Besides our own inquiries into the architectonic antiquities and modern edifices of Italy, which we imagine were made at more expense, and with more assiduity and attention, than any that were ever attempted before, we have consulted Montfaucon, Count Caylus, Count Passeri, Father Gori, and the whole collection af antiquarians who have treated of those matters, without finding a single circumstance that hints at, or alludes to, any such style of decoration.

(B) To enter into any discussion of this subject, would be foreign to our purpose, and would swell our not beyond its proper bounds. Those, therefore, of our Readers, who are desirous of being more fully informed, must consult the learned works of the authors mentioned in our former note; as also those of Dempster, *de Etrur Regal.* Cluverius's *Ital. Antiq.* the Marquis Scipio Maffei, and Francesco Mariani, *passim.*

(C) The Etruscans, by their laws and constitution, gave all possible encouragement to the polite arts and to artists. See *Heracl. Ponticus apud Athen. Deipnosoph. ut et ipse Athen. ibidem,* l. iii, p. 123. l. x. p. 700. They had an admirable quarry of marble near Luna (thought to be that of Carrara), and were famous, from the most remote antiquity for their skill in architecture and masonry. Scip. Maffei, *Orig. Etrus.* p. 15, 16. To them, and not to the Greeks, Tarquin applied for artists, when he determined to build a temple to Jupiter Tarpeius. See Livy, l. 1. Atria, or courts, were first used by the Etruscans. Fest. *in voce* Atrium. By them the Doric Epistylium was first invented, as we learn from Leo Bapt. Alberti, l. vii. c. 6. The noblest amphitheatres in the world were those of the Etruscans. See Maffei, *degli Anfiteatri.* And, lastly, to them the Romans were indebted for that Order which still bears their name; but which, in point of proportion, beauty, and elegance, is so far excelled by the Doric, which it most resembles, that we have refused it a place in our list of the Orders.

(D) The famous *Cloaca maxima,* or great common sewer with ist well-constructed stone arches, of which surprising remains are to be seen at this day, was built by Tarquin I. the fifth King of Rome. The grandeur of this work was never so well understood, says the Marquis Maffei, as when it came to be repaired and cleansed, for which the Censors paid a thousand talents : *Vid.* Scip. Maffei, tom. iii. p. 39-41. Geneva, 1728. See also Dionysius Halicar. *Antiq. Rom.* l. iii. Montesquieu, in his *Causes de la Grandeur, etc. des Romains,* c. i. expressés himself in this remarkable manner concerning the first public work of Rome : « Mais la grandeur de Rome parut bientôt dans ses édifices publics. Les ouvrages « qui ont donné et qui donnent encore aujourd'hui la plus haute idée de sa puissance, ont « été faits sous les Rois. On commençoit déjà à bâtir la ville éternelle. »

(E) Pliny, l. XXXV, c. 14. Juvenal also alludes to this manufacture in these words :

" Aretina nimis ne spernas vasa monemus;
" Lautus erat Tuscis Porsena fictilibus."

(F) For a very ample and learned account of these valuable and innumerable remains of antiquity, see Montfaucon, vol. iii, part 1, p. 142. The Supplement, vol. iii. p. 292. Antiquities of Count Caylus, 5 vols. quarto, à Paris, 1752, pass. Count Jo. Bapt. Passeri, 2 vols. folio; Romæ, 1767. Sir William Hamilton, 2 vol. folio; Naples, 1767. — See also the original vases from whence this last work is drawn; which, having been afterwards purchased by Government, make part of that noble and useful collection of natural and artificial curiosities, which is contained in the British Museum; an institution which reflects great honour on the Legislature of this country.

No. I. — Containing Part of the Designs of the Earl of Derby's House in Grosvenor-Square.

EXPLANATION OF THE PLATES.

PLATE I.

Plans of the Parlour and principal stories as the have been lately altered and newly decorated.

Both these plans exhibit an attempt to arrange the apartments in the French style, which, as hath been observed in a former part of this work, is best calculated for the convenience and elegance of life*. With this view, a large addition has been made to the old wing of the house. The suite of withdrawing-rooms on the principal floor is noble, and well suited to every occasion of public parade. At the same time, care has been taken to render the private apartment commodious. By means of an intersol over the closet and powdering-room, we have introduced a servant's sleeping-room adjoining to this apartment; and a private stair gives convenient access and communication to both stories.

The smallness of the scites upon which most houses in London are built, obliges the artists of this country to arrange the apartments of the Ladies and Gentlemen on two floors. Accordingly, Lords Derby's are here placed on the parlour story. The French, in their great hôtels, with their usual attention to what is agreeable and commodious, would introduce both these apartments upon the principal floor; but this we can only do in our country-houses, where our space is unconfined.

PLATE II.

Section of the Chimney-side of the Anti-room in the principal Story.

The ornaments are all in stucco; and the grounds, both of the cieling and side-walls. are all picked in, with different tints of green, which has a simple and elegant effect. The chimney-piece is of statuary marble, and the girandoles are painted.

PLATE III.

Two Chimney-pieces in the First and Second Withdrawing-rooms, with Glass-Frames over them.

These Chimney-pieces are of statuary marble, and the frames for the glasses are carved in wood and gilt. The figure in the oval at top of the first frame is painted; and the whole is beautifully executed, and has been allowed to have an elegant effect.

PLATE IV.

Section of one End and one Side of the Second Withdrawing-room.

The ornaments of the pilastres, arches, and pannels of the doors, are beautifully painted by Zucchi. Those in the freezes of the room and doors are of stucco, and of wood carved. The magnificent glass-frame in the recess is finely executed in wood and gilt.

PLATE V.

Inside View of the Third and Great Withdrawing-room.

The ornaments of the cieling and entablature are chiefly of stucco gilt, with a mixture of paintings. The grounds are coloured with various tints. The frames for glasses, the pedestals and vases in the niches, and the girandoles on the piers, are of wood gilt. This room is hung with satin, and is undoubtedly one of the most elegant in Europe, whether we consider the variety or the richness of its decoration.

PLATE VI.

Two Chimney-pieces; in the Great Withdrawing-room, and the Countess of Derby's Dressing-room.

The former is finely executed, in statuary marble, inlaid with various coloured *scagliola* and brass ornaments, gilt in *or moulu.* The glass-frame over it is carved in wood, and gilt. The latter is like-wise executed in statuary marble, inlaid with scagliola, in the Etruscan style, both with regard to the form of the ornament, and the peculiarity of the colouring. The glass-frame over it is of wood, carved and coloured in the same manner.

PLATE VII.

Cieling, in the Etruscan Taste, executed in the Countess of Derby's Dressing-room.

The ornaments are partly of stucco, and partly in painting, in the colouring of the Etruscans.

PLATE VIII.

Contains some of the Parts at large of the Finishing and Furniture of the Earl of Derby's House, viz.

The girandoles in the first drawing-room, which are elegantly carved and gilt; with the paintings by Mr. Zucchi.

The pannels of the doors in the third drawing-room, where the ornaments are painted on papier-maché, and so highly japanned as to appear like glass.

The curtain-cornice of the bed-chamber.

The curtain-cornice of the dressing-room, which, with all the other ornaments and furniture of that room, is executed in the Etruscan style; as may be seen from the plate.

No. II. — Containing Part of the Designs of the House of Sir Watkin Williams Wynn, Bart. in St. James's-Square.

EXPLANATION
OF THE
PLATES.

PLATE I.

Plan of the Parlour Story, and principal Floor.

This house, like that described in the preceding Number, is considerably circumscribed with regard to scite; notwithstanding which, great care has been taken to make the apartments spacious, and even magnificent. The eating-room, the music-room, and Sir Watkins's library, below; the two withdrawing-rooms, and Lady Wynn's dressing-room, above; together with the great stair-case, have been thought to merit these appellations : and the others, though of less ample dimensions, are, notwithstanding, sufficiently large, and have been accounted elegant.

PLATE II.

Elevation of the principal Front.

It is not in a space of forty-six feet, which is the whole extent of the elevation, that an architect can make a great display of talents. Where variety and grandeur in composition cannot be obtained, we must be satisfied with a justness of proportion and an elegance of style.

PLATE III.

Plan and Elevation of a Screen-wall between the Court ot the House belonging to the Duke of Leeds and that of Sir Watkin Williams Wynn.

This wall fronts the windows of several of the apartments. It was therefore necessary to make it an object of some beauty and elegance. It is chiefly executed in the stucco known by the name of its inventor, *Liardet;* which has been lately introduced intovery general use, and will not only add new beauty to the exterior appearance of this great Metropolis, but will also contribute to the duration of its buildings.

PLATE IV.

Front of the Offices towards the Court,

Which is built of Portland-stone, and handsomely decorated; because that too is in the view of the apartments.

PLATE V.

Parts at large in the Hall and Eating-room.

PLATE VI.

Cieling of the Eating-room.

PLATE VII.

Cieling of the Music-room.

PLATE VIII.

Plan, Elevation, and Profile, of an Organ in the Music-room.

No. III. — Containing Part of the Designs of Shelburne House in Berkeley-Square.

EXPLANATION
OF THE
PLATES.

PLATE I.

Plan of the principal Floor of Shelburne House.

The scite of this house being more ample than usual in London, it has admitted of a noble suite of apartments both on this floor and on that above. The eating-room, in particular, is of great dimensions, and the gallery is magnificent.

PLATE II.

Elevation of the principal Front towards the Court.

PLATE III.

The Ionic Order in the Front of Shelburne House,

In which the ornament of the frieze is taken from the Temple of Concord at Rome.

PLATE IV.

Section of two Sides of the Porter's Hall.

PLATE V.

Detail at large of the Hall.

In the frieze, a Centaur and Patera are introduced alternately; the former being the crest of the family.

PLATE VI.

Composed Doric Order in the Eating-room, with the Entablature, &c. of one of the Doors.

This capital is antique : the ornament in the frieze is new.

PLATE VII.

Design of a Bridge in imitation of the Aqueducts of the Ancients.

Proposed to be built over a branch of the lake at Bo-wood Park in Wiltshire, one of the seats of the Earl of Shelburne.

PLATE VIII.

Chimney-piece and Table in the Hall of Shelburne House.

No. IV. — Being a Continuation of the Designs of Sion House, a magnificent Seat of the Duke of Northumberland, in the County of Middlesex.

THIS Number is a continuation of the Designs done for his Grace the Duke of Northumberland at Sion House.

The general plan of that house having been published in the first Number of the former Volume, we beg leave to refer the public to that part of our works, for a proper explanation of the following Plates.

Four of these Plates are engraved by Piranesi, and are the largest he has ever attempted in regular architecture. This obligation, from so ingenious an artist, we owe to that friendship we contracted with him during our long residence at Rome, and wich he has since taken every occasion to testify in the most handsome manner.

EXPLANATION OF THE PLATES.

PLATE I.

Section of one Side of the Hall at Sion.

PLATE II.

Detail of the Hall, with the Pedestals for the Figures at large.

PLATE III.

Cieling of the Hall.

PLATE IV.

Two Sections of the Anti-room.

PLATE V.

Ionic Order of the Anti-room, with the rest of the Detail of that Room.

We have formerly mentioned this Ionic capital, as being ornamented in the most splendid manner of which the order is susceptible.

PLATE VI.

Chimney-piece of the Anti-room, with the Pannel over it.

PLATE VII.

Design of a ruinous Bridge for the Garden.

PLATE VIII.

Designs of various Pieces of Furniture,

Which were first invented for particular persons, but are since brought into general use.

No. V. — Containing various Designs of Public and Private Buildings.

EXPLANATION OF THE PLATES.

PLATE I.

Plan, and South Front of the Parisch Church of Mistley in Essex, near the Seat of the Right Honourable Richard Rigby.

PLATE II.

Elevation of one end, and Section through the Church, from East to West.

PLATE III.

South-West View of the Church.

PLATE IV.

Plans of two Stories of the British Coffee-House, with the Elevation towards Cockspur-Street.

PLATE V.

Plan and Elevation of the Gateway and Porter's Lodge of Ashburnham House, in Dover-Street.

PLATE VI.

View of the new Front, towards Bridges-Street of the Theatre-Royal in Drury-Lane.

Both the plain and ornamental parts of this front are executed in Liardet.

PLATE VII.

Inside View of the Theatre-Royal in Drury-Lane, as it appears from the Stage.

Altered and decorated in the year 1775.

PLATE VIII.

Plan and Elevation of a Seat for the Garden of his Grace the Duke of Montagu at Richmond;

In which it was proposed to introduce some antique capitals in his Grace's possession, and also to place within it an ancient Vase and Pedestal.

THE

WORKS IN ARCHITECTURE

OF

ROBERT AND JAMES ADAM, ESQUIRES.

VOLUME III.

Containing the remainder of the Designs, to complete those in the preceding Volumes.

LONDON:

Printed for PRIESTLEY and WEALE, No. 5, HIGH STREET, BLOOMSBURY.

1822.

ADVERTISEMENT.

The Publishers desirous of fulfilling the intention of the late Robert and James Adam, Esqrs. offer to the public the following work, now rendered complete by the addition of a third volume; containing many plates necessary to conclude the series of plans, elevations, and sections, begun and continued in the two first volumes. For instance, the series of designs for Sion-house, one of the mansions of the Duke of Northumberland, which was commenced in the first volume, is now made perfect by the plates contained in the third. The same remark will apply to Luthon house, the seat of the late Earl of Bute, and several other edifices.

The high estimation in which Mr. Robert Adam and his brother were held by Lord Mansfield, and many other noblemen and gentlemen distinguished by their taste in the fine arts, furnishes a convincing proof of their merit.

But the Adams, were not celebrated merely for the classic elegance of their designs, but also in the practical department of their profession, their modes of construction having been applauded by the most eminent architects of their day, and the prefaces to the numbers in which the two first volumes of this work were originally published, are replete with acute observation and classical research.

The work contains one hundred and five plates, twenty-five of which belong to the third volume. Many of the plates are engraved by Zucchi, Pastorini, Cunego, Vivares, and by Piranesi, the friend and admirer of the authors.

In order to give as extended a circulation as possible to a work so necessary to complete the library of all those whose professions are connected with the art of design, the publishers have fixed the price of the work at seven guineas and a half, which, when compared with the selling price of works of much less magnitude and importance, must be considered exceedingly moderate.

E X P L A N A T I O N

OF THE

P L A T E S.

P L A T E I.

View of the front part of the new buildings called Adelphi.

P L A T E II.

Interior view of the library at Sion-house.

P L A T E III.

Geometrical section of the library at Sion-house.

P L A T E IV.

Cerling of the library at Sion-house.

P L A T E V.

Trophies in the anti-room at Sion.

P L A T E VI.

Pavement of the anti-room at Sion.

P L A T E VII.

Ceiling of the anti-room at Sion.

P L A T E VIII.

Furniture at Sion-house.

P L A T E IX.

Furniture at Sion-house.

These nine plates complete the series of designs for Sion house, commenced in the first volume.

P L A T E X.

Detail of Luton fronts.

P L A T E XI.

Drawing-room, glass, and table, assigned for the Earl of Bute.

P L A T E XII.

Plan and elevation of the new screen before the front of the Admiralty.

P L A T E XIiI.

Plan of the principal story of the new building for the university of Edinburgh.

P L A T E XIV.

Design of the east front of the new building for the university of Edinburg.

P L A T E XV.

Design of the south front of ditto.

P L A T E XVI.

Plans of the deputy-ranger's lodge in the Green Park.

P L A T E XVII.

View of the south front of the deputy ranger's lodge.

P L A T E XVIII.

Elevation of the gateway of Shelburne-house.

P L A T E XIX.

Ceiling of the hall at Shelburne-house.

P L A T E XX.

Plan of a pavilion erected for a fête champétre in the garden of the Earl of Derby.

P L A T E XXI.

Interior view of the supper-room and part of the ball-room.

P L A T E XXII.

Inside view of the ball-room and part of the supper-room.

P L A T E XXIII.

Ceiling of the library of Sir W. W. Wynn.

P L A T E XXIV.

Ceiling of Lady Wynn's dressing room.

P L A T E XXV.

Inkstand designed for Sir W. W. Wynn.

THE PLATES

SYON HOUSE

MIDDLESEX

Robert Adam remodelled (1762–1769) the interior of this Jacobean house, originally a Brigetine convent and monastery dating from the mid-fifteenth century, for Hugh Smithson, first duke of Northumberland of the third creation In 1773, he added an entrance screen. Syon House is owned by the present duke of Northumberland.

Plate I.

R. Adam Architect 1769

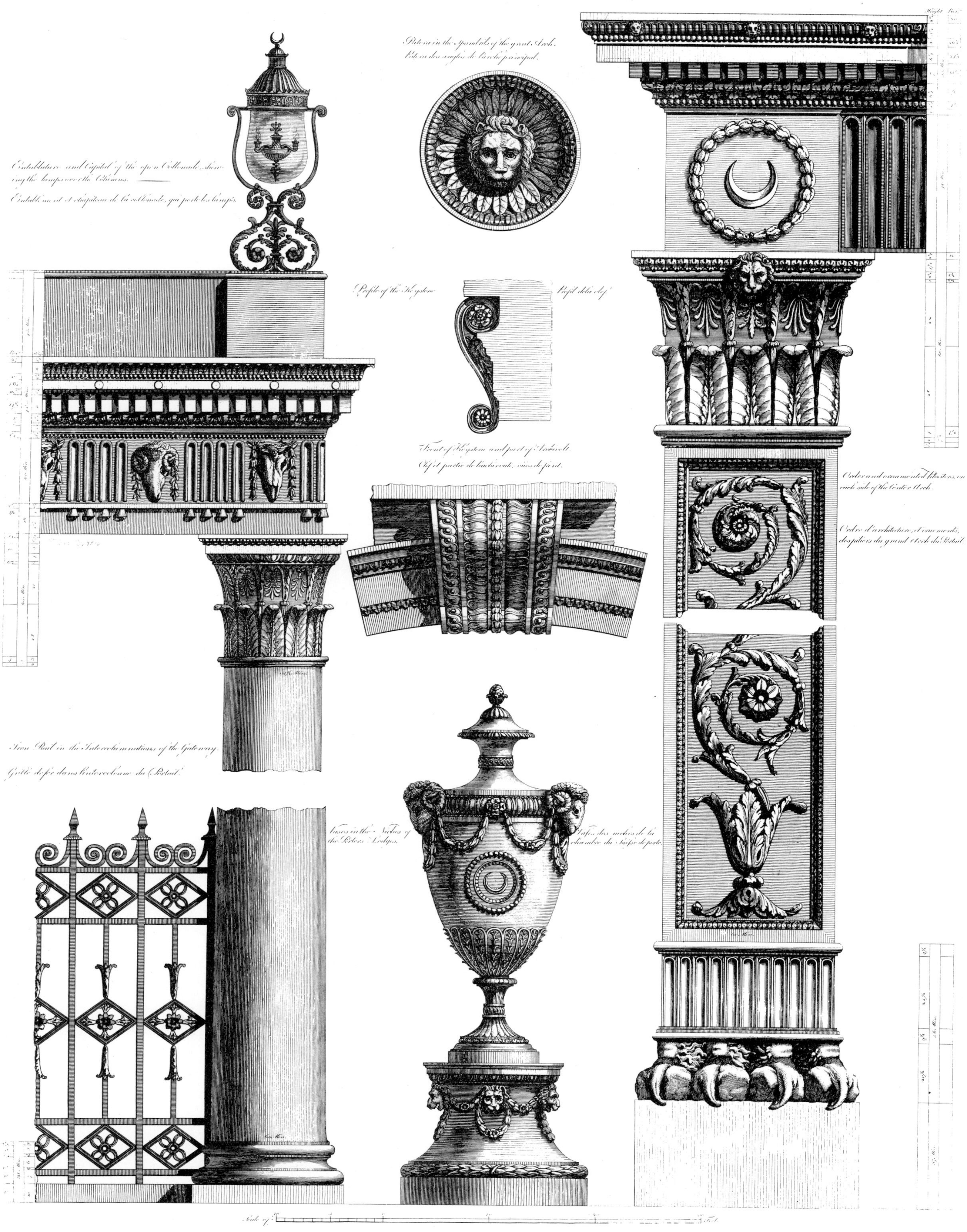
Entablature and Capital of the open Collonade, shewing the lamps over the Columns.
Entablement et chapiteau de la collonade, qui porte les lamps.
Patera in the Spandrils of the great Arch.
Patera des angles de l'arche principal.
Profile of the Keystone
Profil de la clef
Front of Keystone and part of Archivolt.
Clef et partie de l'archivolte, vües de front.
Order and ornamented Pilasters, on each side of the Center Arch.
Ordre d'architecture, et ornements, des piliers du grand Arch du Portail.
Iron Rail in the Intercolumnations of the Gateway.
Grille de fer dans l'intercolonne du Portail.
Vases in the Niches of the Porters Lodges.
Vases des niches de la chambre du Suisse de porte.

Perspective View of the Bridge at Sion.
Perspective du pont du Chateau de Sion.

Geometrical Elevation of a Bridge proposed to be built over the River in the Garden at Sion. ——
Elevation geometrique d'un Pont a construire sur la riviere qui passe dans les jardins du Chateau de Sion.

Plan of the Foundations of the Bridge.
Plan des fondements du Pont.

Plan of the Carriage and Footways of the Bridge.
Plan de la chaussé et des trottoirs du Pont.

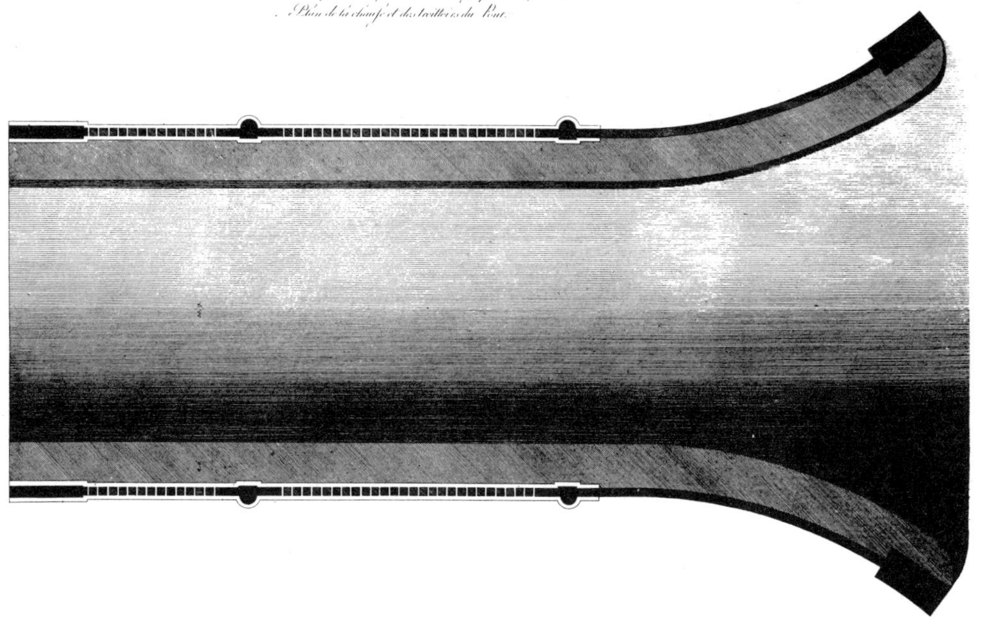

Scale of Feet

R. Adam Architect 1761.

T. Miller sculp.

Vol. II

Design of a Ruinous Bridge for the Garden at Sion. — No. IV. — Dessein d'un Pont delabré pour le Jardin à Sion. — Pl. VII.

Rt. Adam Architect 1768. — Scale of Feet — Published as the Act directs 1778 — T. Vivares sculpsit.

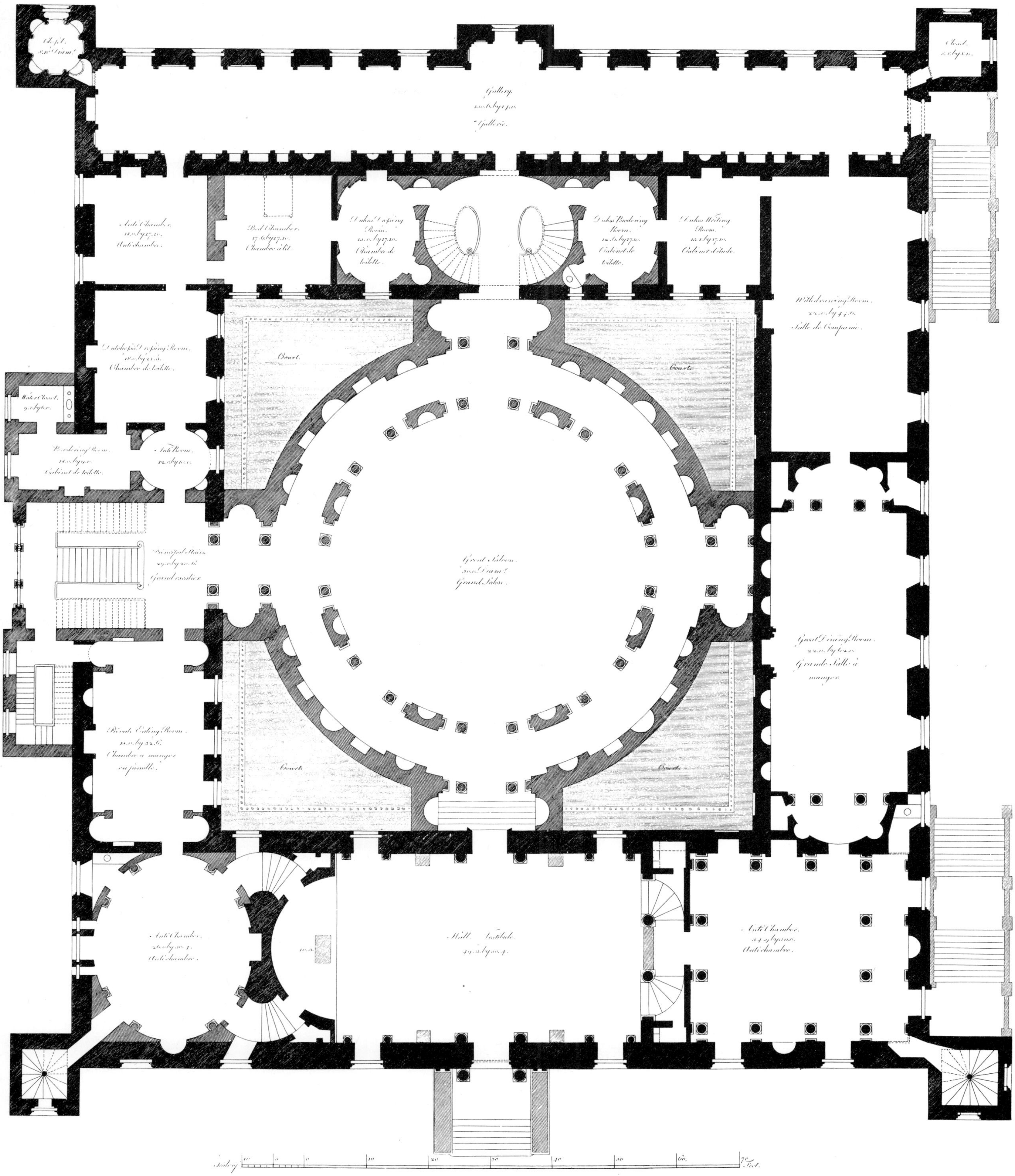

Plan of the principal Story of Sion House.

Plan du premier étage du Chateau de Sion.

R. Adam Architect 1761. D. Mazell sculp.

Section of one side of the Hall at Sion

Coupe de la Salle d'Entrée à Sion

Rt Adam Architect 1761

Published as the Act directs 1778

Eques J. B. Piranesi sculpt Romæ

No. I.

Section of one End of the Hall, next to the great Apartment. *Coupe du Vestibule au Côté des grands Apartements.*

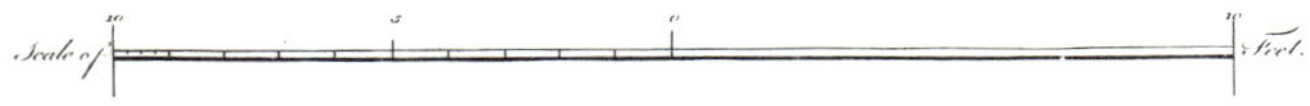

Section of one End of the Hall, next to the private Apartment. Coupe du Vestibule au Côté des Apartements particuliers.

T. White Sculp.

Vol. II

Ceiling of the Hall.

N.º IV

Plafond de la Salle d'Entrée

Pl. III

R.d Adam Architect [inv]it.

Published as the Act directs 1778

Eques J.B. Piranesi incidit Rom

Vol. I. No. I. Plate VII

Order of the lower range of Windows in the Hall.
Ordre de la rangée inférieure des fenêtres du Vestibule.

Trophies in the pannels under the Windows of the Hall.
Trophées sur les panneaux sous les Fenêtres du Vestibule.

Entablature of the upper range of Windows in the Hall, the Cornice of which goes quite round the Room.
Entablement de la rangée supérieure des fenêtres du vestibule, dont la corniche règne tout autour de la chambre.

Vase in the pannels on each side of the Door going into the Anti Room of the great Apartment.
Vase sur les panneaux de chaque coté de la porte de l'anti-chambre du grand Appartement.

Consol which supports the Columns.
Console qui supporte les Colonnes.

Profile of the Columns and Consols.
Profil des Colonnes et de leurs consoles.

[illegible] Sculp.

Vol II.
Detail of the Hall at Sion.
N° IV
Detail de la Salle d'Entrée à Sion.
Pl II
Doric Order of the Hall.
Ordre Dorique de la Salle d'Entrée.
Frame round Basreliefs in the sides of the Hall.
Bordure autour des Bas-reliefs dans les cotés de la Salle.
Frame round Basrelief at the end of the Hall.
Bordure autour des Basreliefs au bout de la Salle.
Front & Profile of the Dressings of the Attic Windows in the Hall.
Elévation et Profil des décorations des Fenêtres Attiques dans la Salle.
Pedestals between the Doors & Windows.
Piédestaux entre les Portes et les Fenêtres.
Scale of 12 6 0 1 2 3 4 Feet
Pedestal in the Great Circular Nich.
Piédestal dans le Grande Niche Circulaire.
Published as the Act directs 1778.
R. Adam Architect 1761.
Pinnie incidit.

Section of the Window side of the Anti-room. *Coupe de l'Antichambre à Sion du coté des Fenêtres.*

Scale of 10 9 8 7 6 5 4 3 2 1 0 10 *Feet*

Section of the door side of the Anti room *Coupe de l'Antichambre à Sion du coté de la Porte.*

R. Adam Architect 1761 Published as the Act directs 1778. Eques J. B. Piranesi incidit Rom.

Profile of the Pannell.
Profil du Panneau.

Chimney Piece of the Anti-room, with the Pannell over it.

Cheminée de l'Antichambre avec le Panneau au dessus.

Scale of 12 6 0 1 2 3 4 5 Feet

Rt Adam Architect 1763. *Published as the Act directs 1778.* *Dom: Cunego incidit Romæ*

R.t Adam Architect 1761. Published as the Act directs 1778. Eques J. B. Piranesi incidit Rom.

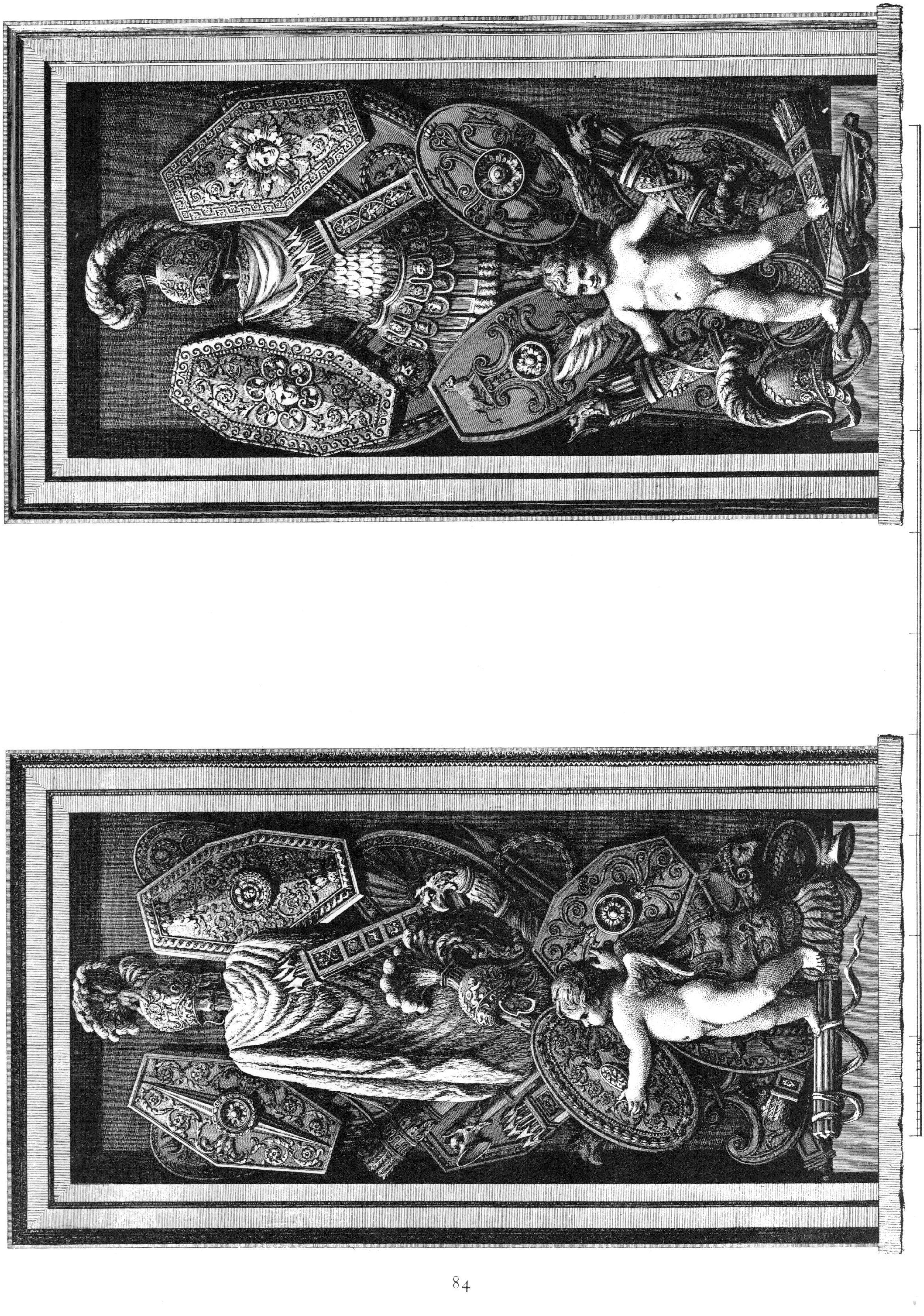

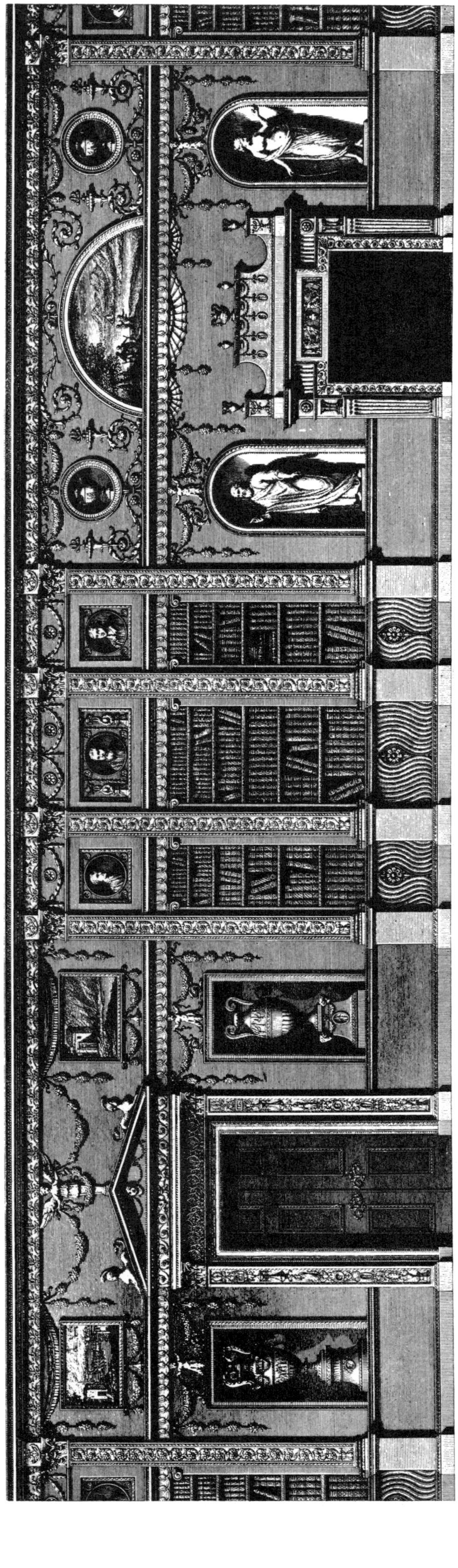

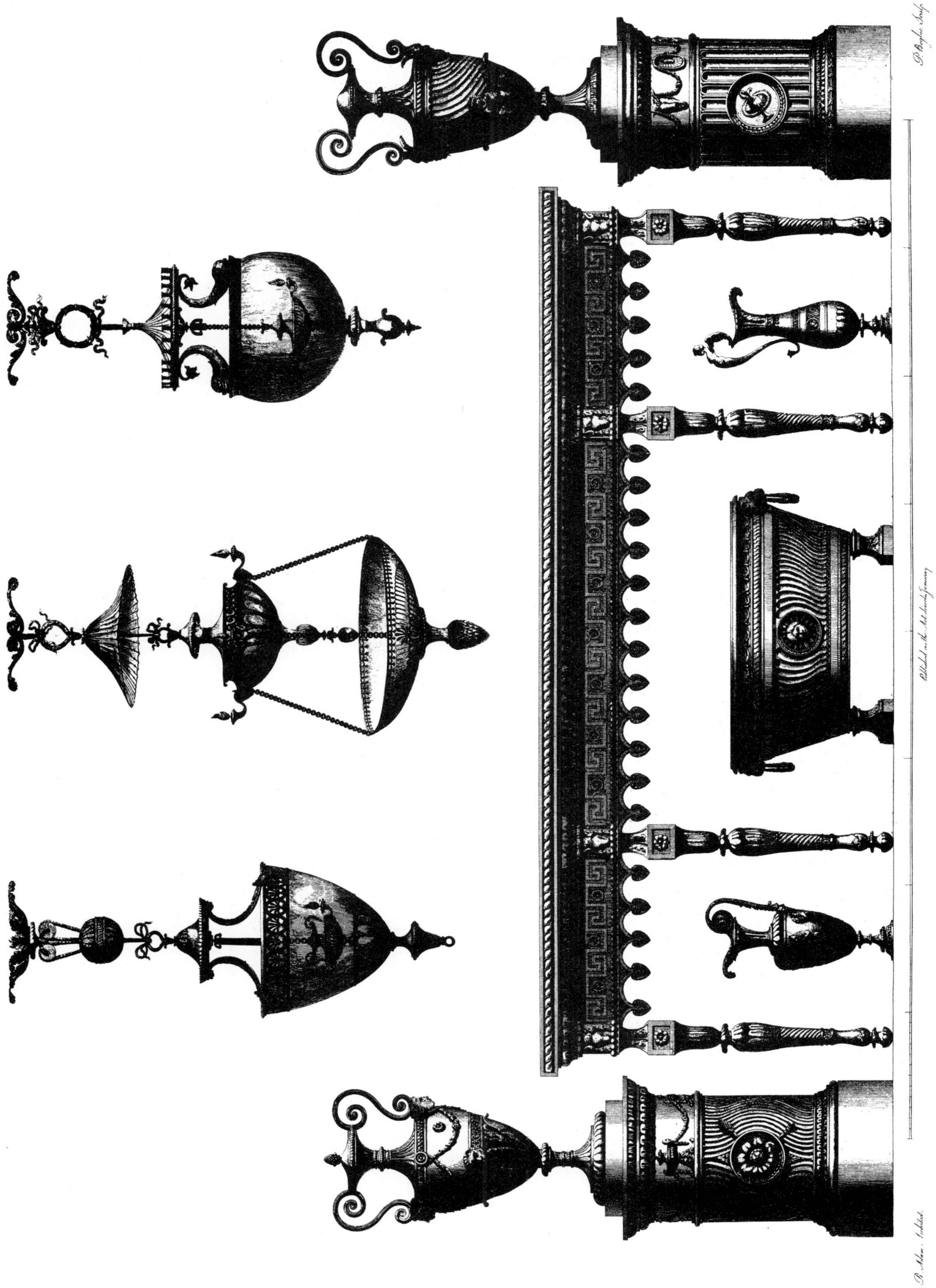
R. Adam Architect.
P. Begbie Sculp

KENWOOD HOUSE

MIDDLESEX

Adam undertook extensive alterations to both the interior and exterior of this late seventeeth century house for his Scottish compatriot, William Murray, first earl of Mansfield, between 1767 and 1769. Kenwood is currently owned by the Greater London Council under the Iveagh Bequest.

Vol. I. | N.º II. | Plate II.

R. Adam Architect 1764.

View of the south Front of the Villa at Kenwood.

Published as the Act directs 1st February 1774.

Vue de la Villa de Kenwood au midi.

Zucchi del. Pastorini sculp.

N° II.

Plate III.

Elevation of the North Front of Kenwood, towards the Court.

Elévation de la Façade au Nord de la Villa de Kenwood donnant sur la Cour.

Elevation of the South Front of Kenwood, towards the Gardens.

Elévation de la Façade au midi, de la Villa de Kenwood donnant sur les Jardins.

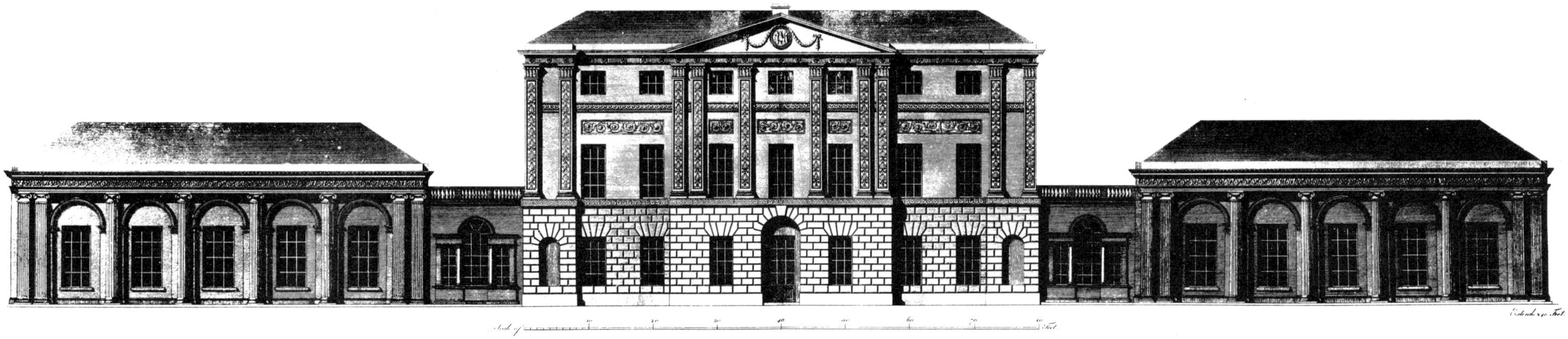

Published as the Act directs

T. Miller Sculp.

Vol: I.
Exterior Order of the Body of the House towards the Garden.
Ordre extérieur du corps de logis sur le Jardin.
Nº II.
Exterior Order of the New Wing.
Ordre extérieur de la nouvelle aile.
Plate IV.
Soffite of the Corona.
Plafond de la Corone.
String which seperates the Attic from the Bed Chamber Story.
Cordon qui sépare le premier du second étage.
String which seperates the Basement from the Bed Chamber Story.
Impost & Archivolt of the new Wing

N.° II.

Plate I

General Plan of Lord Mansfield's Villa at Kenwood.

Plan général de la Villa du Lord Mansfield à Kenwood.

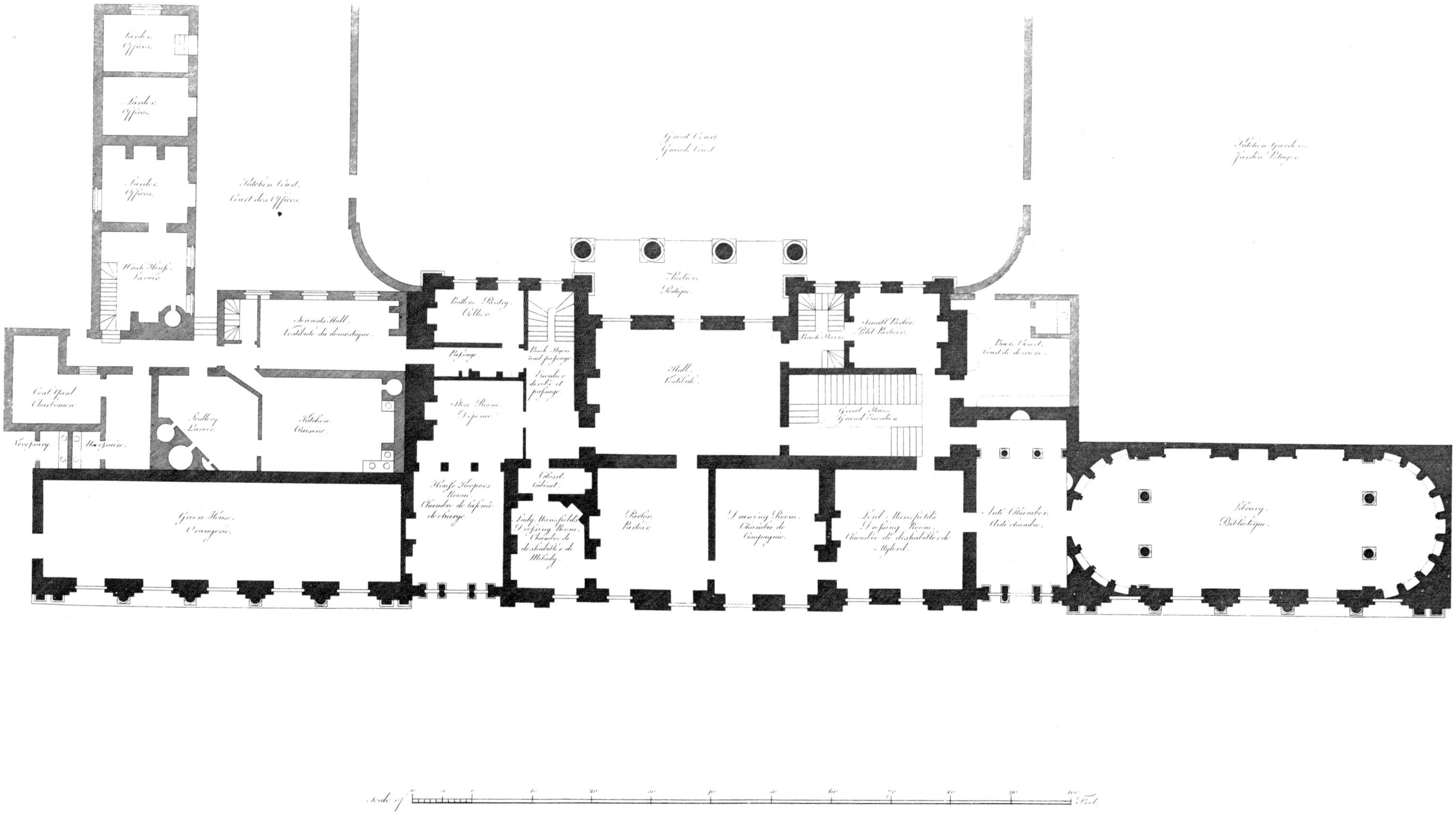

Published as the Act directs 1st Feb. 1774.

C. White Sculp.

Section of one of the sides of the Great Room, or Library at Kenwood.

Coupe latérale de la Grand Salle, ou Bibliotèque de la Villa de Kenwood.

Scale of 10 5 0 10 20 30 Feet.

R. Adam Architect 1767. | Published as the Act directs 5th February 1774. | J. Zucchi sculp. London

Section of one end of the Library or great Room at Kenwood.

Coupe d'un des bouts de la Bibliotèque à Kenwood.

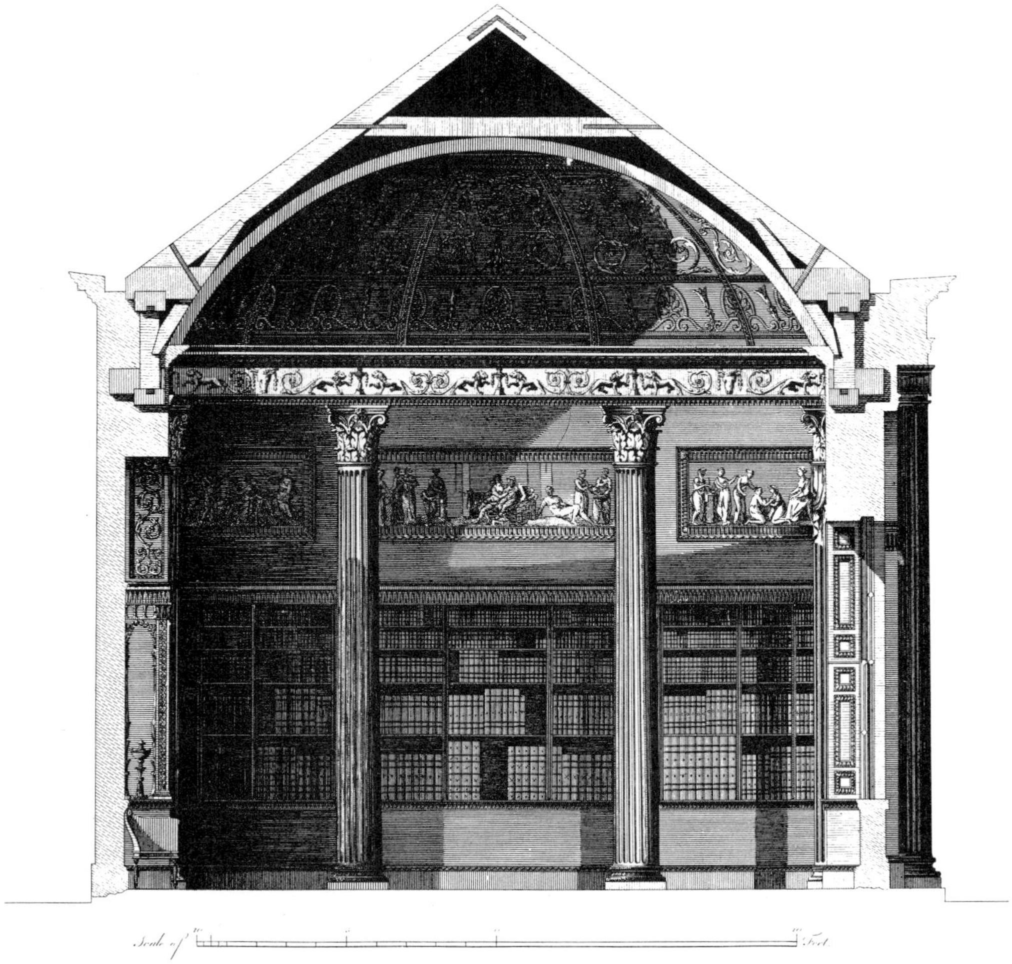

Design of the Chimney for the Library or great Room at Kenwood.

Dessein de la Cheminée de la Bibliotèque à Kenwood.

R. Adam Architect 1767

Published as the Act directs 1st February 1774.

J. Roberts Sculp.

Design of the Ceiling of the Library or Great Room, at Kenwood.

Dessein du plafond de la Bibliotéque de la Villa, de Kenwood.

Scale of 10 5 0 10 20 30 40 50 Feet.

R. Adam Architect, 1767. Published as the Act directs 4th February 1774. B. Pastorini Sculp.

Vol: I.
Nº II.
Plate VIII
Design of the Pier Glasses in the great room
Dessein des Glaces dans les trumeaux du Salon
Pier Glass in the Parlour
Glace dans les Trumeaux du Parloir
Pier Glass in the Dining room
Glace dans les Trumeaux de la Salle à manger
Design of the side Board table in the Dining room
Dessein du Buffet ou table à vaisselle de la Salle à manger
Scale for the Glasses
Scale of Feet
R. Adam Architect
Published as the Act directs 5th February 1771
P. Begbie Sc.

DERBY HOUSE

GROSVENOR SQUARE

LONDON

Derby House was decorated by Adam for Edward, Lord Stanley, later twelfth earl of Derby, between 1773 and 1774. It was demolished in 1862.

Plans of the parlour and principal floors. Vol II, No I, Pl I. Engraved by Robert Blyth. *p. 100.*

Section of the ante-room. Vol II, No I, Pl II. Engraved by Joseph Record. *p. 101.*

Two sections of the second drawing room. Vol II, No I, Pl IV. Engraved by Joseph Record. *p. 102.*

Two chimney pieces, one from the first drawing room and one from the second drawing room. Vol II, No I, Pl III. Engraved by Joseph Record. *p. 103.*

View of the third drawing room. Vol II, No I, Pl V. Engraved by Benedetto Pastorini. *p. 104.*

Two chimney pieces, one from the third drawing room and one from the countess of Derby's dressing room. Vol II, No I, Pl VI. Engraved by Giuseppe Carlo Zucchi. *p. 105.*

Ceiling of the countess of Derby's dressing room. Vol II, No I, Pl VII. Engraved by Benedetto Pastorini. *p. 106.*

Furniture for Derby House. Vol II, No I, Pl VIII. Engraved by Benedetto Pastorini. *p. 107.*

Plan of a pavilion in the garden at the Oaks in Surrey for a fête champêtre. Vol III, Pl XX. Engraved by John Roberts. *p. 108.*

View of the supper room and part of the ballroom in the pavilion. Vol III, Pl XXI. Engraved by James Caldwall and Charles Grignion. *p. 109.*

View of the ballroom and part of the supper room in the pavilion. Vol III, Pl XXII. Engraved by James Caldwall. *p. 110.*

Plan of the Parlor Story of the Earl of Derby's House in Grosvenor Square.
Plan du rez de Chaussée de la Maison du Comte de Derby dans le Quarré de Grosvenor.

Plan of the principal Story.
Plan du principal Etage.

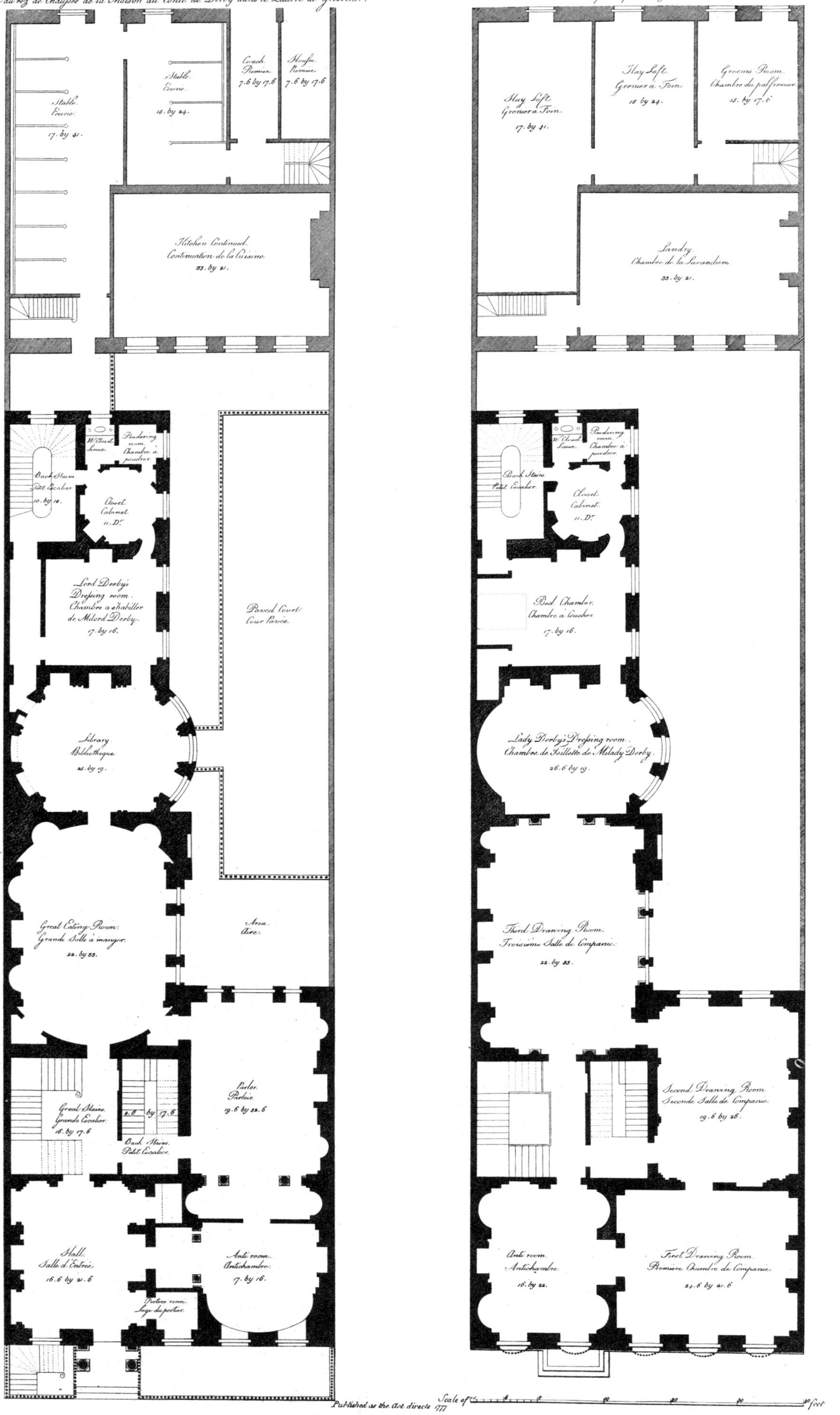

R. Adam Architect 1773 | Published as the Act directs 1777 | R. Blyth incidit

Vol: II. | N.° I. | Plate II

Section of the Chimney-side of the Antichamber in the Principal Story. | *Coupe du coté de la Cheminée de l'Antechambre au Principal Étage.*

Scale of 10 feet

R.d Adam Architect 1773. | Published as the Act directs 1777. | Jos.h Record incidit.

Section of one End of the second Drawing-room. — *Coupe d'un Bout de la seconde Salle d'Assemblée.*

Section of one Side of the second Drawing-room. — *Coupe d'un Coté de la seconde Salle d'Assemblée*

Scale of feet

Adam Architect 1775. *Published as the Act directs 1777.* *Jos.ʰ Record incidit.*

Chimney piece of Statuary Marble in the first Drawing room with the Glass & Frame over it.
Chambranle de Marbre Statuaire dans la premiere Salle d'Assemblée, avec la Glace, et sa Bordure au dessus.

Chimney piece of Statuary Marble in the second Drawing room with the Glass & Frame over it.
Chambranle de Marbre Statuaire dans la seconde Salle d'Assemblée, avec la Glace et sa Bordure au dessus.

Scale of 10 feet

R. Adam Architect 1773.

Published as the Act directs 1777.

Record incidit.

N° I.

Inside View of the third Drawing-room at the Earl of Derby's House in Grosvenor Square.

Vüe de l'Interieur de la troisieme Chambre d'Assemblée dans la Maison du Comte de Derby.

R. Adam Architect 1773.

Published as the Act directs 1777.

B. Pastorini incidit.

Vol. II. | N.º I. | Plate VI.

Chimney-piece of Statuary Marble for the third Drawing-room, ornamented in Scagliola & Or Moulu, with the Glass frame over it.
Chambranle de Marbre Statuaire pour la troisieme Salle d'Assemblée orné en Scagliola et Or Moulu, avec la Glace et sa Bordure au dessus.

Chimney-piece for the Countess of Derby's Etruscan Dressing room, of white Marble inlaid with Ornaments of Scagliola in the Etruscan taste, with the Glass frame over it.
Chambranle pour la Chambre Etrusque à Toillette de Madame la Comtesse de Derby de Marbre blanc marquetté avec ornemens de Scagliola dans le goût Etrusque, avec la Glace et sa Bordure au dessus.

Scale of 12 6 0 1 2 3 4 5 feet

R. Adam Architect 1773 | Published as the Act directs 1777 | J. Zucchi Sculp. London.

Vol: II.

Design of a Cieling in the Etruscan taste executed in the Countess of Derby's Dressing room.

Nº. I.

Dessein d'un Plafond dans le gout Etrusque executé dans la Chambre a toilette de la Comtesse de Derby.

Plate VII.

Scale of 1 2 3 4 5 10 15 20 *feet*

Rt. Adam Architect 1773.

Published as the Act directs 1777.

B. Pastorini incidit.

Vol: II.
Plate VIII.
Girandoles in the first Drawing room
Girandoles dans la premiere Salle d'Assemblée
Curtain Cornice of the Bed Chamber
Corniche aux Rideaux de la Chambre à coucher
Nº I.
Curtain Cornice of the Etruscan room
Corniche aux Rideaux de la Chambre Etrusque
Girandole in the Nich of the Etruscan room
Girandole dans la Niche de la Chambre Etrusque
Girandoles in the Etruscan room
Girandoles dans la Chambre Etrusque
Folding Doors of the third Drawing room
Portes à deux Battons pour la troisieme Salle d'Assemblée
Folding Doors for the Etruscan room
Portes à deux Battons pour la Chambre Etrusque
Top of a Commode in the Countess of Derby's Dressing room
Dessus d'une Commode dans la Chambre à Toilette de Mad.me la Comtesse de Derby
Front of a Commode in the Countess of Derby's Dressing room
Facade d'une Commode dans la Chambre à Toilette de Mad.me la Comtesse de Derby
Rt. Adam Architect 1774
Scale of
feet
Published as the Act directs 1777.
B. Pastorini incidit

Plan of a Pavilion erected for a **FÊTE CHAMPÊTRE** *in the Garden of the Earl of Derby at the Oaks in Surry, the 9th of June, 1771.*

Plan d'un Pavillon érigé pour une **FÊTE CHAMPÊTRE** *dans le Jardin du Comte de Derby à Oaks en Surry, le 9me de Juin, 1774.*

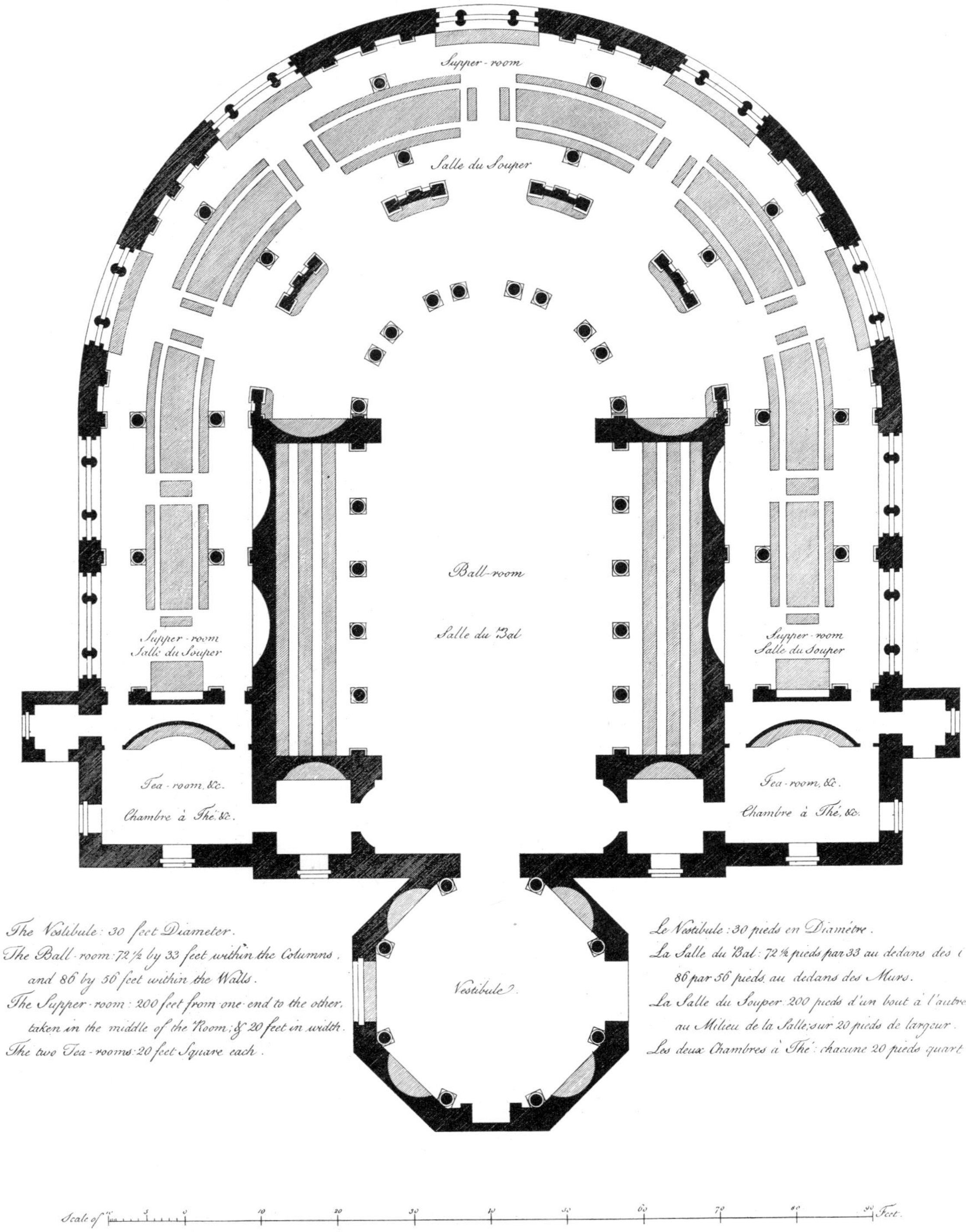

The Vestibule: 30 feet Diameter.
The Ball-room: 72½ by 33 feet within the Columns, and 86 by 56 feet within the Walls.
The Supper-room: 200 feet from one end to the other, taken in the middle of the Room; & 20 feet in width.
The two Tea-rooms: 20 feet Square each.

Le Vestibule: 30 pieds en Diamétre.
La Salle du Bal: 72½ pieds par 33 au dedans des (
86 par 56 pieds au dedans des Murs.
La Salle du Souper: 200 pieds d'un bout à l'autre au Milieu de la Salle; sur 20 pieds de largeur.
Les deux Chambres à Thé: chacune 20 pieds quart

Robert Adam Architect. *Published as the Act directs.* *John Roberts incidit*

Robert Adam Architect. | Jas. Caldwall & C. Grignion Sculpserunt.

Inside view of the Supper-room & part of the Ball-room in a Pavilion erected for a **FÊTE CHAMPÊTRE** *in the Garden of the Earl of Derby at the Oaks in Surry, the 9.th of June. 1771.*

Vüe intérieure de la Salle du Souper, et d'une partie de celle du Bal, dans un Pavillon érigé pour une **FÊTE-CHAMPÊTRE** *donnée par le Comte de Derby dans son Jardin à Oaks en Surry, le 9.me de Juin. 1774.*

Published as the Act directs

Robert Adam Architect

Inside view of the Ball-room in a Pavilion erected for a **FÊTE CHAMPÊTRE** *in the Garden of the Earl of Derby at the Oaks in Surry, the 9th of June, 1774.*

Published as the Act directs

Jas. Caldwall Sculpsit

Vüe intérieure de la Salle du Bal dans un Pavillon érigé pour une **FÊTE CHAMPÊTRE** *donnée par le Comte de Derby dans son Jardin à Oaks en Surry, le 9me de Juin, 1774.*

THE WILLIAMS WYNN HOUSE

ST. JAMES'S SQUARE

LONDON

Robert Adam rebuilt and redecorated this town house for the Welsh baronet, Sir Watkin Williams Wynn, between 1772 and 1774. It is currently the headquarters of the Distillers Company.

Elevation of the House of Sir Watkin Williams Wynn Baronet in St. James's Square.

No. II.

Elévation de la Maison du Mons.r le Chevalier Watkin Williams Wynn dans la Place de St. Jacques.

Scale of 10 5 0 10 20 30 feet

Adam Architect 1772.

Published as the Act directs 1777.

Jn.o Roberts incid.t

Vol. II. Plan of the Parlor Story of Sir Watkin Williams Wynn's House in St. James's Square. No. II. Plan du Rez de Chaussée de la Maison du Monr. le Chevalier Watkin Williams Wynn dans la Place de St. Jacques. Pl. I

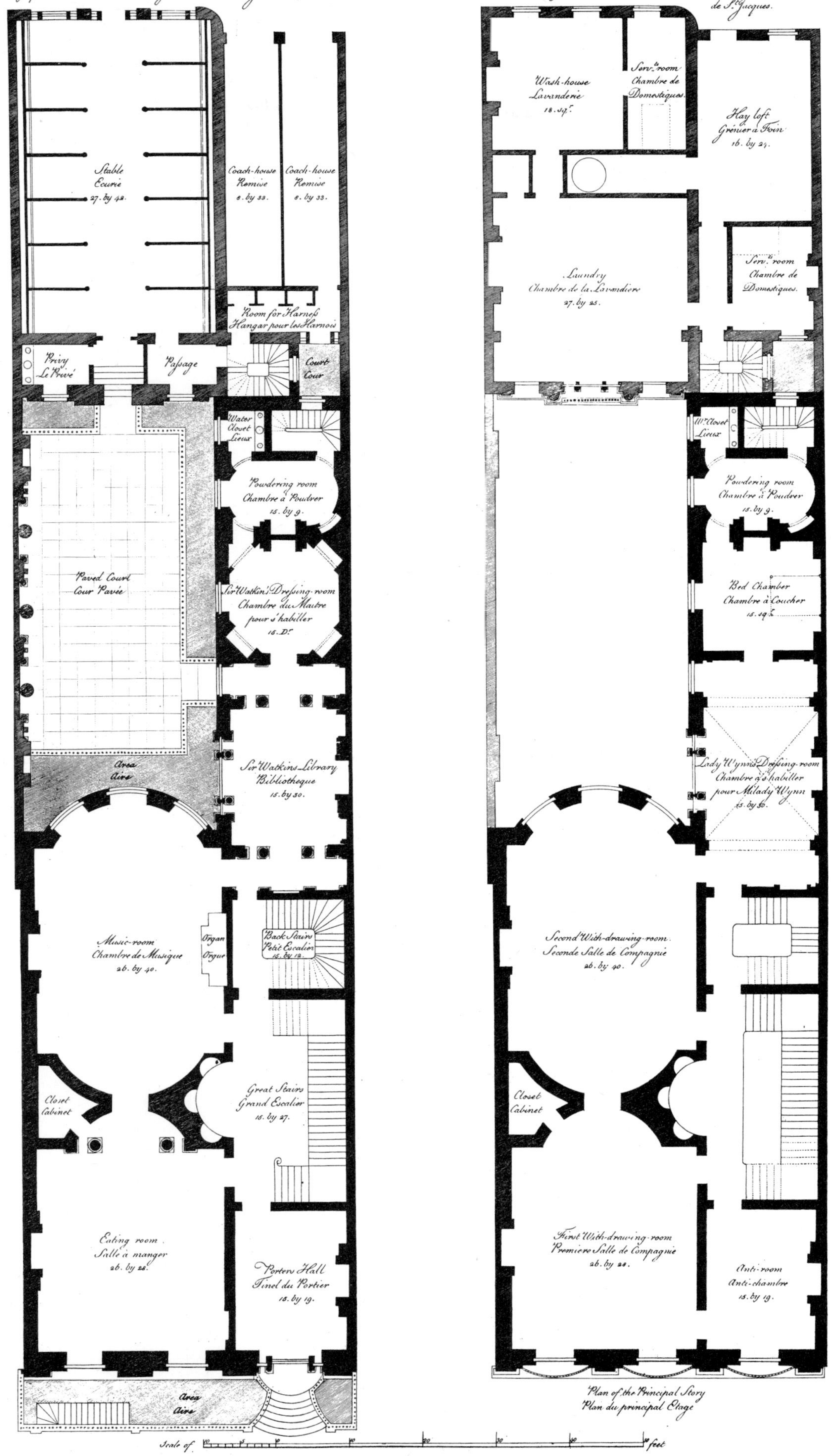

R. Adam Architect 1772 — Published as the Act directs 1777 — Norval incidit

Ceiling of the Eating-Room. | Plafond de la Salle à Manger.

R.d Adam Architect 1772. | Published as the Act directs 1777. | Roe incidit

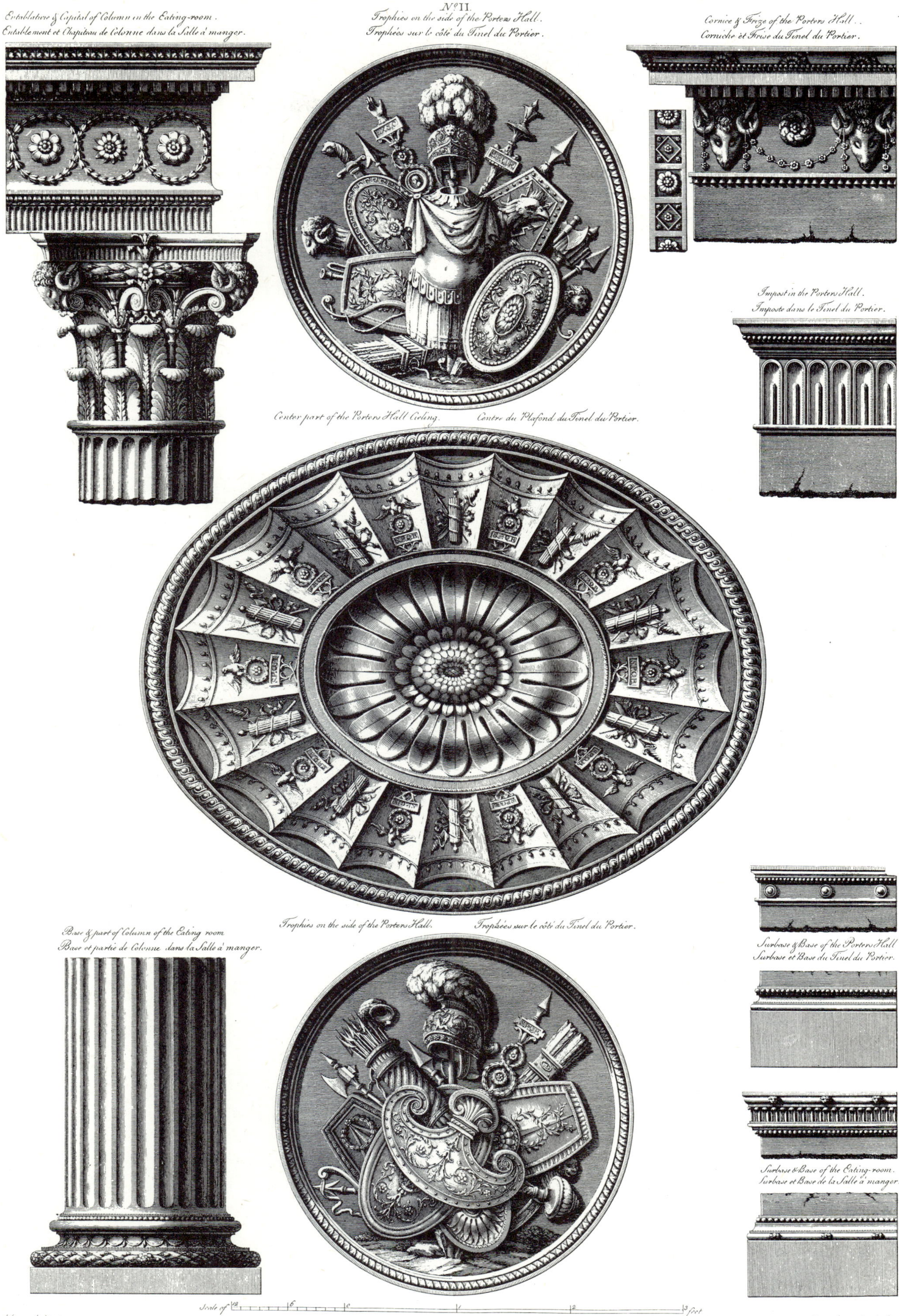

R. Adam Architect 1773

Published as the Act directs 1777.

J. Zucchi Sculp. London

Scale of 10 feet

R. Adam Architect 1773. Published as the Act directs 1777. Dom: Cunego incidit Rom.

Cieling of the Music Room. — *Plafond de la Salle de Musique*

Scale of Feet

Rᵗ Adam Architect 1773. — *Published as the Act directs 1777* — *T. Morris incidit*

South Elevation of the Wall in the back Court.

Elévation meridionale du Mur dans l'arrière Cour.

Plan of the Wall.
Plan du Mur.

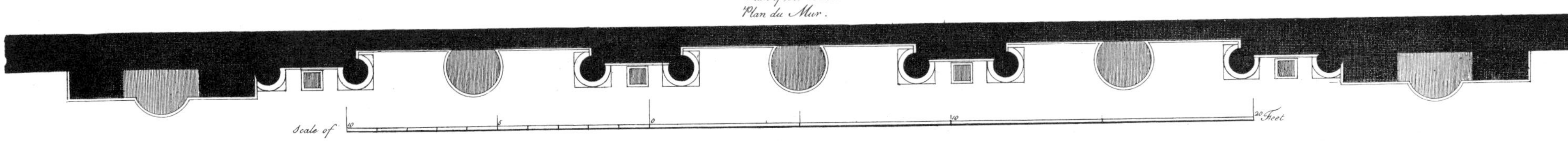

Rt. Adam Architect 1772.

Published as the Act directs 1777.

Dom. Cunego incidit Romæ

Elevation of the Offices towards the back Co

Elévation des Offices vers l'arrière Cour.

R.t Adam Architect 1772. Publish'd as the Act directs 1777. T. Vivarez sculpsit

SHELBURNE HOUSE

BERKELEY SQUARE

LONDON

Adam built this house for William Petty, second earl of Shelburne, later first marquess of Lansdowne, between 1762 and 1768. Renamed Lansdowne House, much of it was demolished in 1929 and then rebuilt on a smaller scale. It is currently owned by the Lansdowne Club, although the original dining room is preserved intact at the Metropolitan Museum, New York.

Elevation of the gateway. Vol III, Pl XVIII. No engraver indicated. *p. 124.*

Elevation of the principal front. Vol II, No III, Pl II. Engraved by Thomas White. *p. 125.*

Order of the principal front. Vol II, No III, Pl III. Engraved by Thomas Vivares. *p. 126.*

Plan of the principal floor. Vol II, No III, Pl I. Engraved by Charles White. *p. 127.*

Two sections of the hall. Vol II, No III, Pl IV. Engraved by Peter Mazell. *p. 128.*

Ceiling of the hall. Vol III, Pl XIX. No engraver indicated. *p. 129.*

Details from the hall. Vol II, No III, Pl V. Engraved by Alexander Finnie. *p. 130.*

Details from the dining room. Vol II, No III, Pl VI. Engraved by Thomas Vivares. *p. 131.*

Table and chimney piece from the hall. Vol II, No III, Pl VIII. Engraved by James Caldwall. *p. 132.*

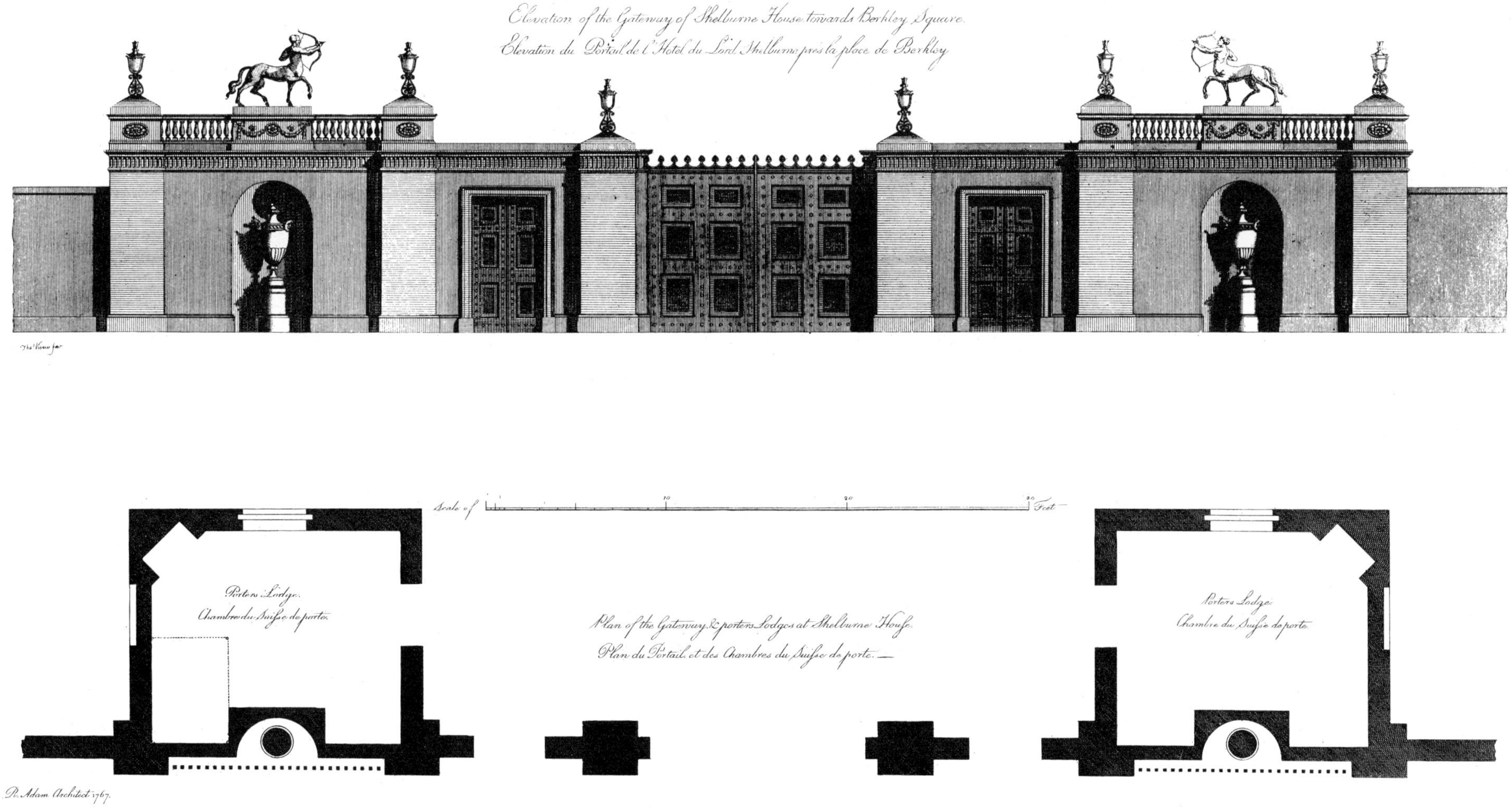
Elevation of the Gateway of Shelburne House towards Berkley Square
Elevation du Portail de l'Hotel du Lord Shelburne pres la place de Berkley
Tho. Vivares sc.
Scale of 10 20 30 Feet
Porters Lodge
Chambre du Suisse de porte
Plan of the Gateway & porters Lodges at Shelburne House
Plan du Portail et des Chambres du Suisse de porte
Porters Lodge
Chambre du Suisse de porte
R. Adam Architect 1767

Elevation of Shelburne House in Berkeley Square.

Elevation de l'Hôtel de Shelburne dans la Place de Berkeley.

Scale of 10 5 0 10 20 30 40 50 Feet.

R.d Adam Architect 1765.   Published as the Act directs 1778.   T. White incidit.

The Exterior Order of the Front.

Ordre exterieur de la Façade.

R. Adam Architect 1765. Scale of 6 0 1 2 3 Feet. Published as the Act directs 1778. T. Vivares incidit.

Plan of the Principal Story of Shelburne House in Berkeley Square.

Plan du principal Etage de l'Hôtel de Shelburne dans la Place de Berkeley.

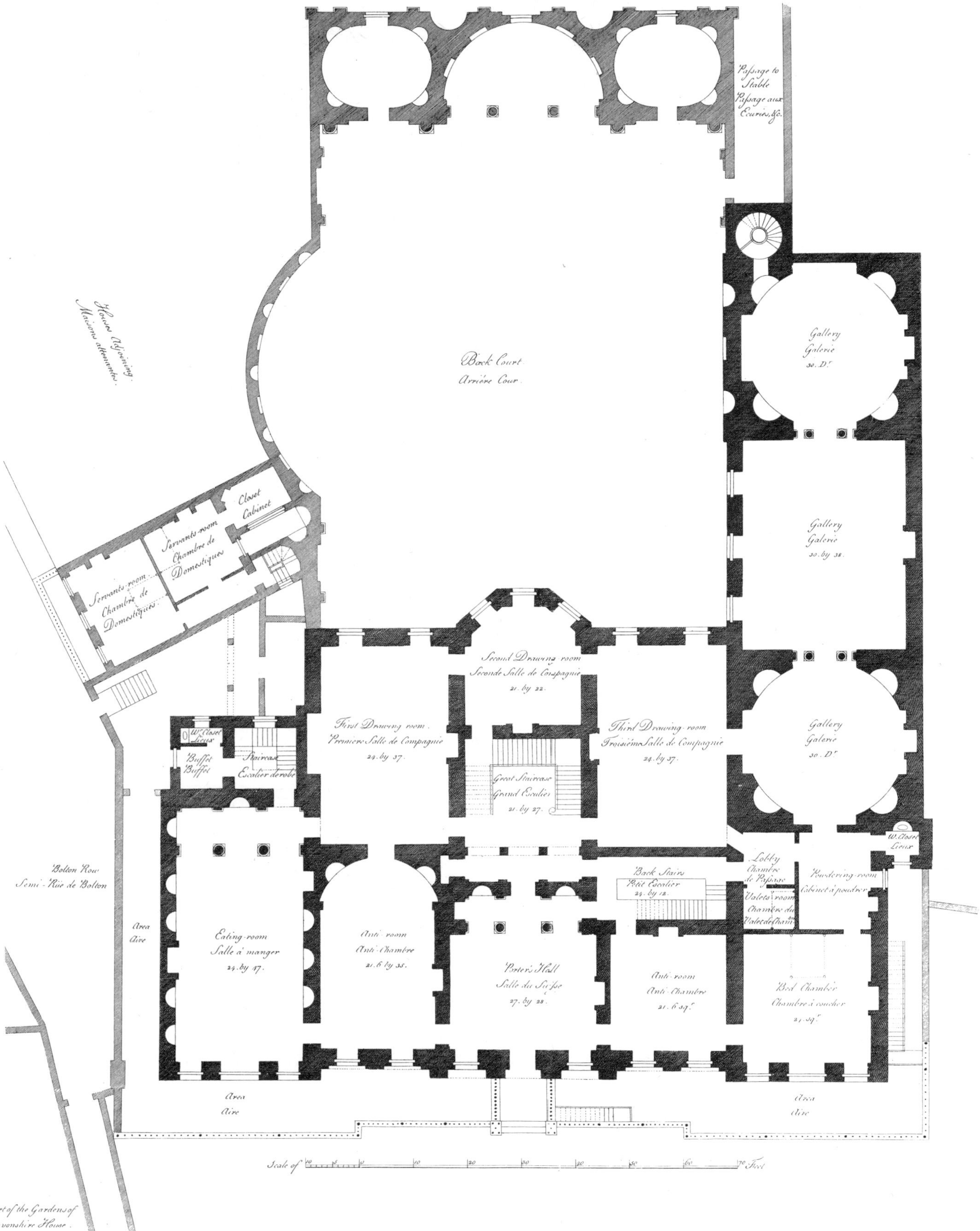

R. Adam Architect 1763. | Publish'd as the Act directs 1778. | C. White sculpt.

Section of two sides of the Porters Hall. Coupe laterale de deux cotés de la Salle du Suisse.

Scale of 10 9 8 7 6 5 4 3 2 1 0 10 Feet.

Rᵗ Adam Architect 1766. Published as the Act directs 1778. P. Mazell incidit.

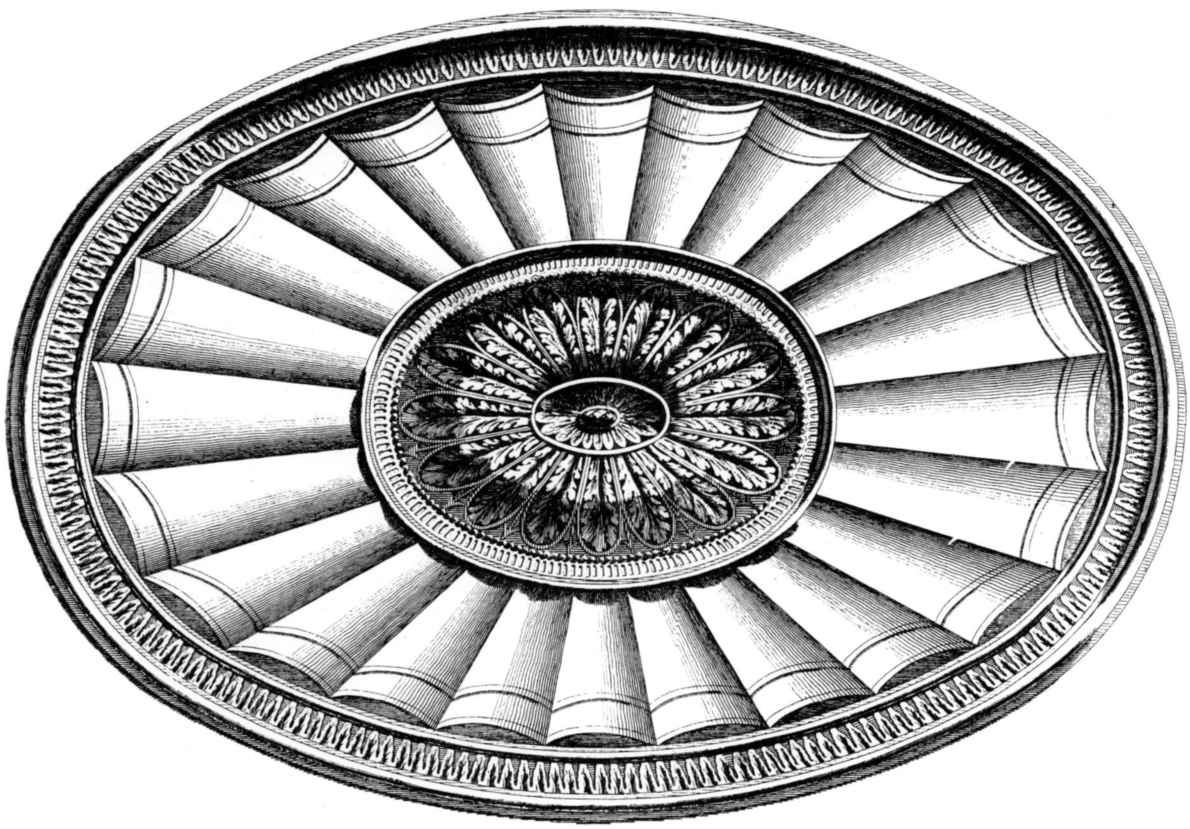

Doric Order in the Porters Hall.

Ordre Dorique dans la Salle du Suisse.

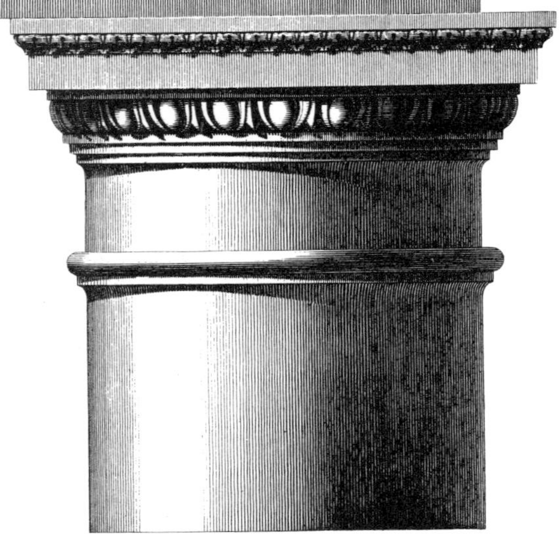

Entablature of the Doors in the Porters Hall.
Entablement des Portes dans la Salle du Suisse.

Base & Surbase Mouldings.
Moulures des Base et Surbase.

Scale of 12 6 0 Feet

'Adam Architect 1766. Published as the Act directs 1778. Alex: Finnie incidit

Composed Doric Order in the Eating-room.

Ordre Dorique composé dans la Salle à manger.

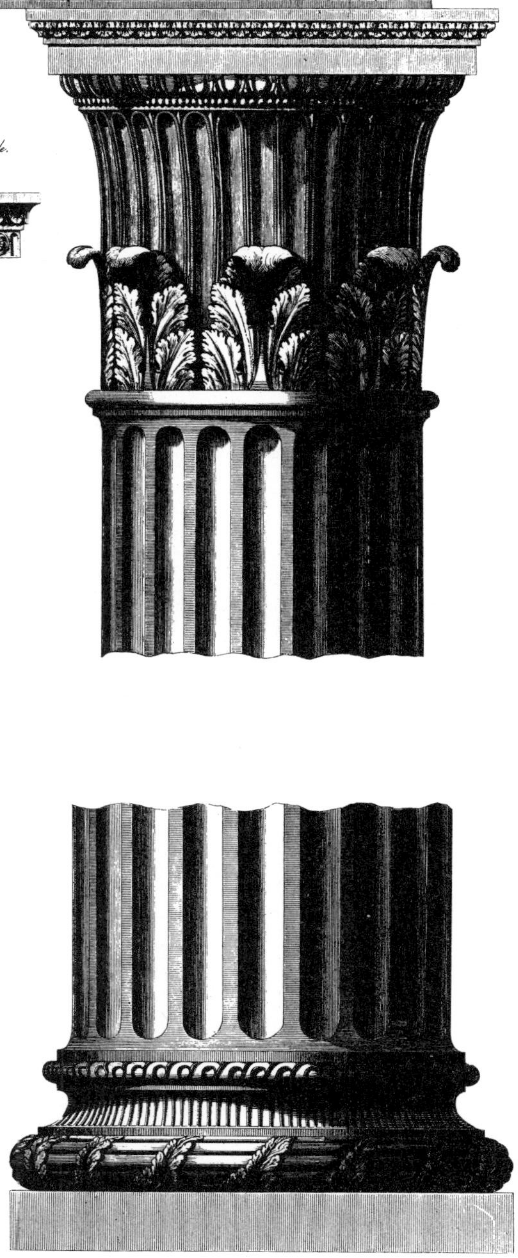

Entablature of Doors in the Eating-room

Entablement des Portes dans la Salle à manger.

Profile of the console.

Profil du console.

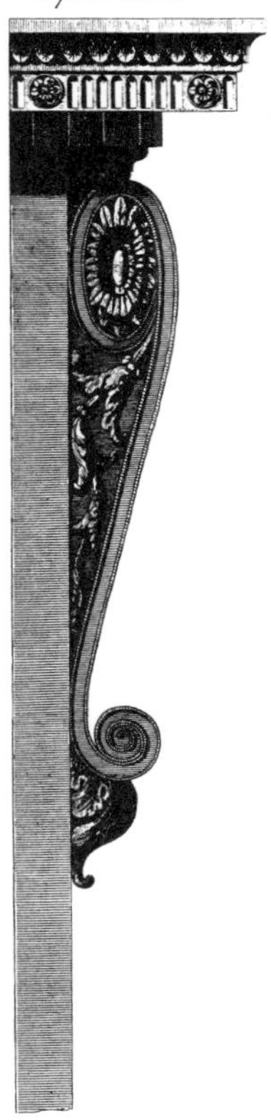

Scale of 12 6 0 Feet

..Adam Architect 1768. | as the Act directs 1778. | T. Vivarez incidit.

Table in the Hall. — *Table dans la Salle du Suisse.*

Scale of 12 6 0 1 2 3 4 *Feet.*

Chimney piece in the Hall — *Chéminée dans la Salle du Suisse.*

R. Adam Architect 1768. — *Published as the Act directs 1778.* — *Caldwall incidit.*

LUTON PARK HOUSE

BEDFORDSHIRE

Adam built Luton Park House for John Stuart, third earl of Bute, between 1767 and 1775. Alterations were carried out in 1816 (by Sir Robert Smirke) and in 1903, but most of Adam's interior decoration had already been destroyed by fire in 1843.

Elevation of the principal front. Vol I, No III, Pl III. Engraved by F. Miller. *p. 134.*

Elevation of the east front. Vol I, No III, Pl IV. Engraved by James(?) Newton. *p. 135.*

Elevations of the north and south fronts. Vol I, No III, Pl V. Engraved by Thomas Vivares. *p. 136.*

Details from the fronts. Vol III, Pl X. Engraved by Giuseppe Carlo Zucchi. *p. 137.*

Details from the salon and the stairs. Vol I, No III, Pl VI. Engraved by Giuseppe Carlo Zucchi. *p. 138.*

Plan of the principal floor as designed originally by Robert Adam. Vol I, No III, Pl I. Engraved by Charles White. *p. 139.*

Plan of the principal floor as built with Robert Adam's own alterations. Vol I, No III, Pl II. Engraved by Charles White. *p. 140.*

Ceiling of the countess of Bute's dressing room. Vol I, No III, Pl VII. Engraved by Benedetto Pastorini. *p. 141.*

Furniture for Luton Park House. Vol I, No III, Pl VIII. Engraved by Benedetto Pastorini. *p. 142.*

Furniture for the earl of Bute. Vol III, Pl XI. No engraver indicated. *p. 143.*

Elevation of the Principal or West front of Luton Park House. One of the Seats of the Earl of Bute. —

Elévation de la Facade principale, vers l'Ouest de la Maison du Parc de Luton, un des Chateaux du Comte de Bute.

R. Adam Architect 1771 Published as the Act directs June 1774 T. Miller Sculp.

Elevation of the East Front of Luton Park House towards the River

Elévation de la Façade Orientale du Château de Luton Parc vers la Rivière

Scale of 10 20 30 40 50 60 70 80 90 100 Feet

Published as the Act directs, June 1774

R. Adam Architect 1767   Newton Sculp

No. III.

Elevation of the North End of Luton Park House.

Élévation du Bout Septentrional de la Maison de Luton Parc.

Extends 149 Feet.

Elevation of the South End of Luton Park House.

Élévation du Bout Méridional de la Maison de Luton Parc.

Scale of 10 20 30 40 50 60 70 80 90 100 Feet.

Published as the Act directs, June 1771.

R. Adam Architect

J. Zucchi Sculp. Londini

Vol: I
Cornice, Frize, and Capital for the Screens in Saloon.
Corniche, Frize, et Chapiteau pour les Écrans dans le Salon.
Nº III.
Moulding and Frize round the Saloon.
Moluse et Frize autour du Salon.
Plate VI.
Upper Cornice of Staircase
Corniche superieure de l'Escalier
Surbase in Saloon.
Surbase dans le Salon.
Base for the Columns in Saloon.
Base pour les Colonnes dans le Salon.
Base in Saloon.
Base dans le Salon.
R. Adam Architect 1770.
Published as the Act directs, June 1774.
J. Zucchi Sculp. London.

No. III.

Plan of the Principal Story of Luton Park House, in Bedfordshire, first intended to be Executed.

Plan de Rez de Chaussée de la Maison de Luton Parc, dans le Comté de Bedford, selon la première intention de l'exécuter.

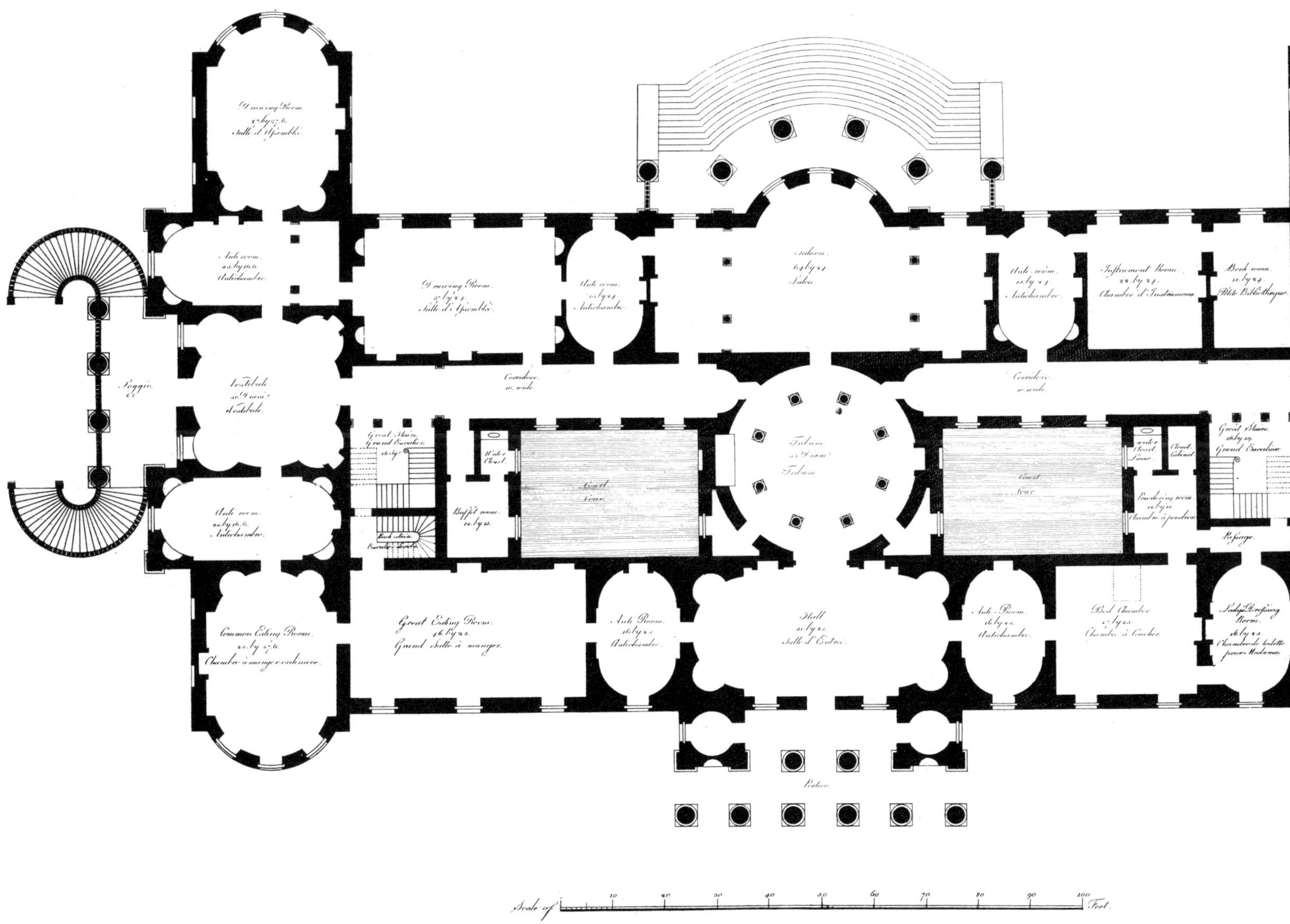

Published as the Act directs, June 1774.

R. Adam Architect 1771.

C. White Sculp.

Vol. I

Nº III.

Plate II

Principal Story of the Earl of Butes House, at Luton Park in Bedfordshire.

Plan de Rez de Chaussée de la Maison de Comte de Bute, a Luton Parc, dans le Comté de Bedford.

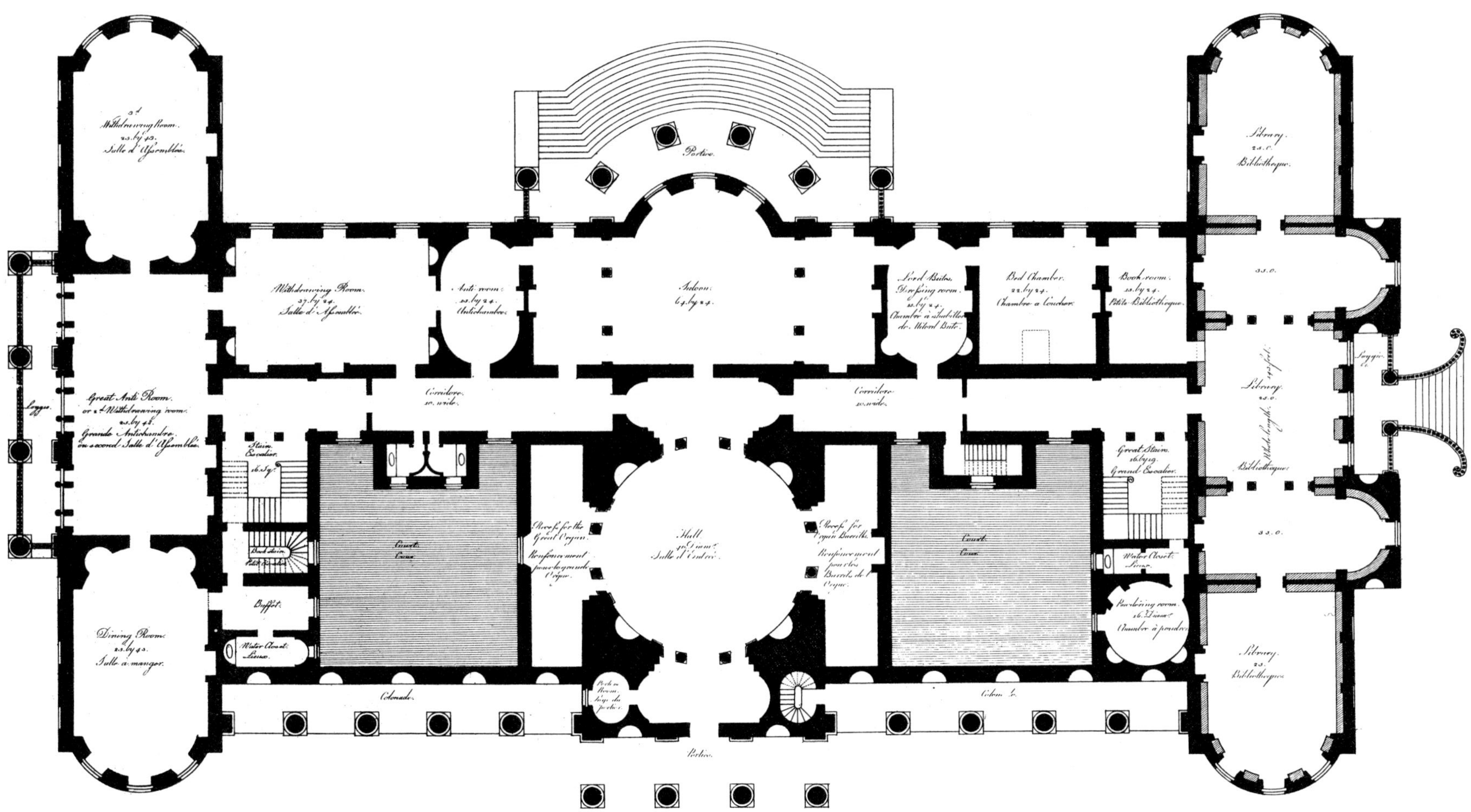

Scale of 10 20 30 40 50 60 70 80 90 100 Feet.

Published as the Act directs June 1774.

R. Adam Architect 1772.

C. White Sculp.

No III

Plate VII

Design of the Ceiling of Lady Bute's Dressing Room.

Dessein du Plafond de la Chambre de Toilette de la Comtesse de Bute.

Scale of 5 10 15 20 Feet

Adam Architect 1769. Published as the Act directs, June 1774. B. Pastorini sculp.

Curtain Cornice executed in two Antichambers & two Dressing rooms at Luton.
Corniche de Rideaux des deux Antichambres et deux Chambres de Toilette à Luton.
Nº III
Curtain Cornice for the Withdrawing Room.
Corniche des Rideaux de la Salle d' Assemblée.
Plate VIII.
Curtain Cornice for the Saloon
Corniche des Rideaux du Salon
Two Bronzes executed in Italy in the Style of Mich. Angelo. The Branches for Candles & the pedestals were added in London, according to this Design.
Deux Bronzes exécutés en Italie dans le Style de Michel Ange. les Branches pour les Chandelles et les Piedestaux, ont été ajoutés à Londres d'après ce dessein.
Stove executed in Brass & Steell, for the Library at Luton in 1764
Grille a feu, éxecutée en cuivre jaune et acier pour la Bibliotheque à Luton, en 1764.
Another pair of Bronzes in the same Style, placed in the Niches of the Withdrawing Room, at Luton.
Deux autres Bronzes dans le même Style, placées dans les Niches de la Salle d' Assemblée à Luton.
R. Adam Architect.
Published as the Act directs June 1771
B. Pastorini Sculps

THE ADELPHI

THE STRAND

LONDON

The Adelphi project, which consisted of two blocks of houses parallel to the Thames and two more perpendicular to the river, was undertaken entirely on the Adam brothers's initiative and constructed between 1768 and 1774. The only buildings to survive the demolition of the Adelphi in 1936 are the current No. 7 Adam Street and the Royal Society of Arts building in John Adam Street.

View of the south front. Vol III, Pl I. Engraved by Benedetto Pastorini. *p. 146.*

THE SOCIETY OF ARTS

JOHN ADAM STREET

LONDON

The Society for the Encouragement of Arts, Manufactures and Commerce, now the Royal Society of Arts, was founded in 1754, and Adam built the house between 1772 and 1774 as part of the Adelphi project.

Elevation of the principal front. Vol I, No IV, Pl IV. Engraved by Thomas Vivares. *p. 147.*

Plan of the principal floor and of the adjoining secretary's house. Vol I, No IV, Pl III. Engraved by Robert Blyth. *p. 148.*

THE ADMIRALTY SCREEN

WHITEHALL

LONDON

One of Adam's first commissions after settling in London, the Admiralty screen was built between 1759 and 1761. It exists today with only minor alterations.

View of the screen. Vol I, No IV, Pl I. Engraved by Domenico Cunego. *p. 149.*

Plan and elevation of the screen. Vol III, Pl XII. Engraved by F. Patton. *p. 150.*

THE CHELSEA HOSPITAL COMMISSION

WHITEHALL

LONDON

Adam remodelled this house at No. 1 Whitehall as a board-room for the paymaster-general and the commission for the Chelsea Hospital, of which he was clerk of the works. It has been demolished.

Elevation of the principal front. Vol I, No IV, Pl II. Engraved by Robert Blyth. *p. 151.*

CARLTON HOUSE

PALL MALL

LONDON

Augusta of Saxe-Gotha, Princess Dowager of Wales, commissioned Adam to make extensive alterations to Carlton House, but his designs were never executed. The house was finally demolished in 1827–1829 and replaced by Nash's well known Carlton House Terrace.

Plan and elevation of the gateway. Vol I, No V, Pl I. Engraved by John Miller. *p. 152.*

Details from the gateway. Vol I, No V, Pl III. Engraved by Domenico Cunego. *p. 153.*

Order of the gateway. Vol I, No V, Pl II. Engraved by Domenico Cunego. *p. 154.*

THE DEPUTY RANGER'S LODGE

GREEN PARK

LONDON

Robert Adam built this house in 1768. It was demolished in 1851.

View of the south front. Vol III, Pl XVII. Engraved by Thomas Vivares. *p. 155.*

Plans of the parlour and first floors. Vol III, Pl XVI. Engraved by John Roberts. *p. 156.*

VIEW of the *SOUTH FRONT* of the New Buildings called ADELPHI, formerly DURHAM YARD, and also that part of the Cities of LONDON & WESTMINSTER which extends along the RIVER THAMES to the MONUMENT.

The above Print exhibits the Royal Terras, the Houses, and Openings of the Streets leading to the Strand; Together with the Wharfs, Arcade, and entrances to the Subterraneous Streets, and Warehouses of the Adelphi, which is a private Undertaking of Mess.rs ADAM, designed by them, and begun to be carried into Execution in July 1768, Being so contrived as to keep the Access to the Houses, level with the Strand, and distinct from the Traffic of the Wharfs and Warehouses.

Publish'd according to Act of Parliament

Vol. I. Nº IV. Plate IV.

Elevation of the House of the Society for the Encouragement of Arts, Manufactures & Commerce, situated in John Street, Adelphi.

Elévation de la Maison de la Société pour l'Encouragement des Arts, des Manufactures, et du Commerce, situeé dans la Rue de Jean, aux Adelphi.

R. & J. Adam Architect 1772.

T. Vivares Sculp.

No. IV.

Plan of the Principal Story of the Society's House, & of the Secretary's House adjoining.

Plan du principal Étage de la Maison de la Société, et de celle du Secrétaire qui lui est contigue.

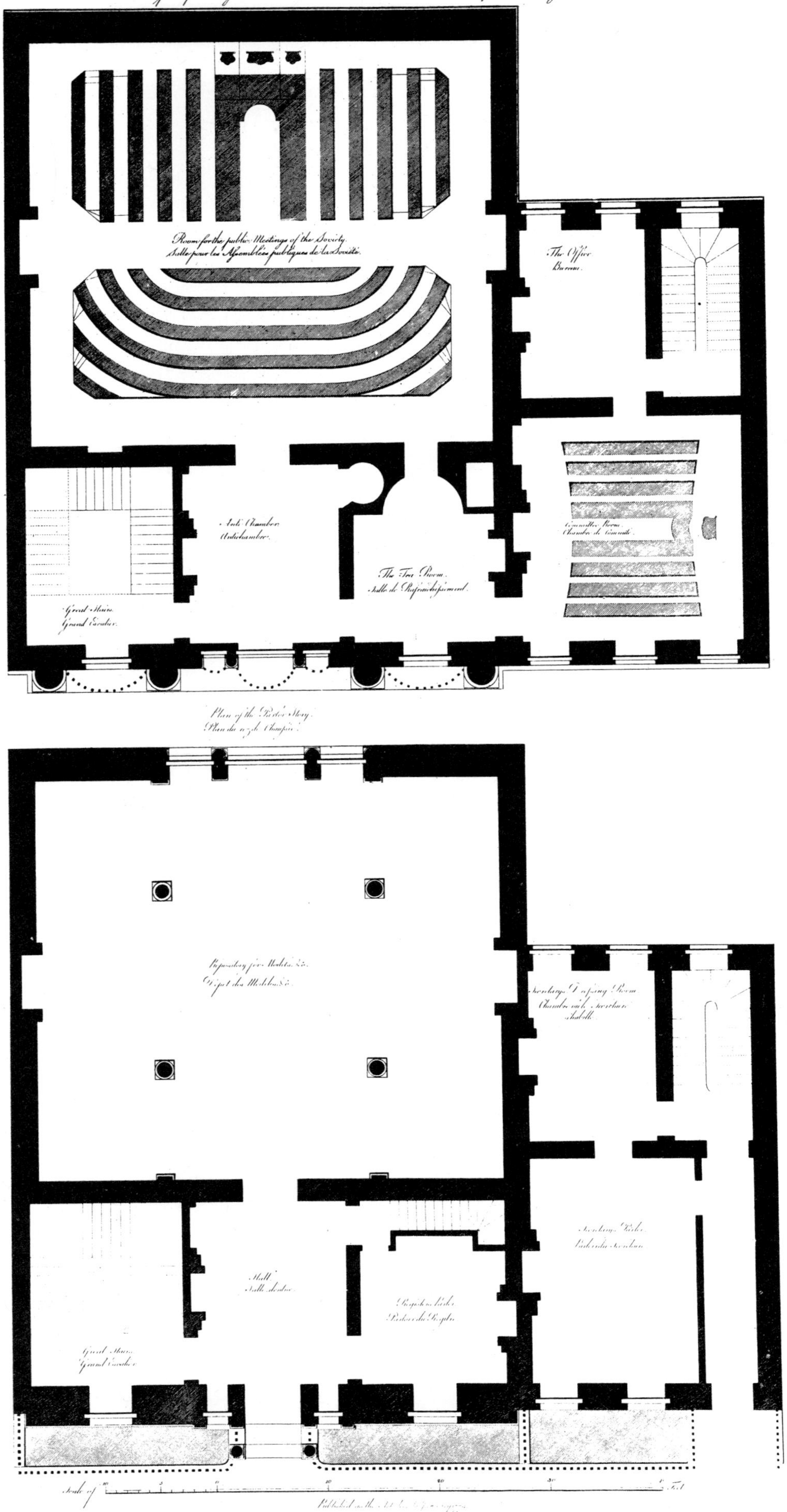

D. Cunego Sculpsit.

View of Part of Whitehall, Shewing the Admiralty Office, with the new Gateway, designed & executed in the year 1760, & also a part of the Horse Guards, &c.

Vue d'une partie de Whitehall, représentant l'Amirauté, avec la nouvelle Porte Cochère, dessinée et executée dans l'année 1760, et aussi une partie du Batiment fait pour la Garde à Cheval, &c.

This Plan and Elevation of the New **SCREEN or GATEWAY** Executed before the Front of the

Admiralty,

Is humbly Inscribed To the Right Honourable The Lords Commissioners of the Admiralty

By Their Lordships Most Obedient and Very Humble Servant

Robert Adam.

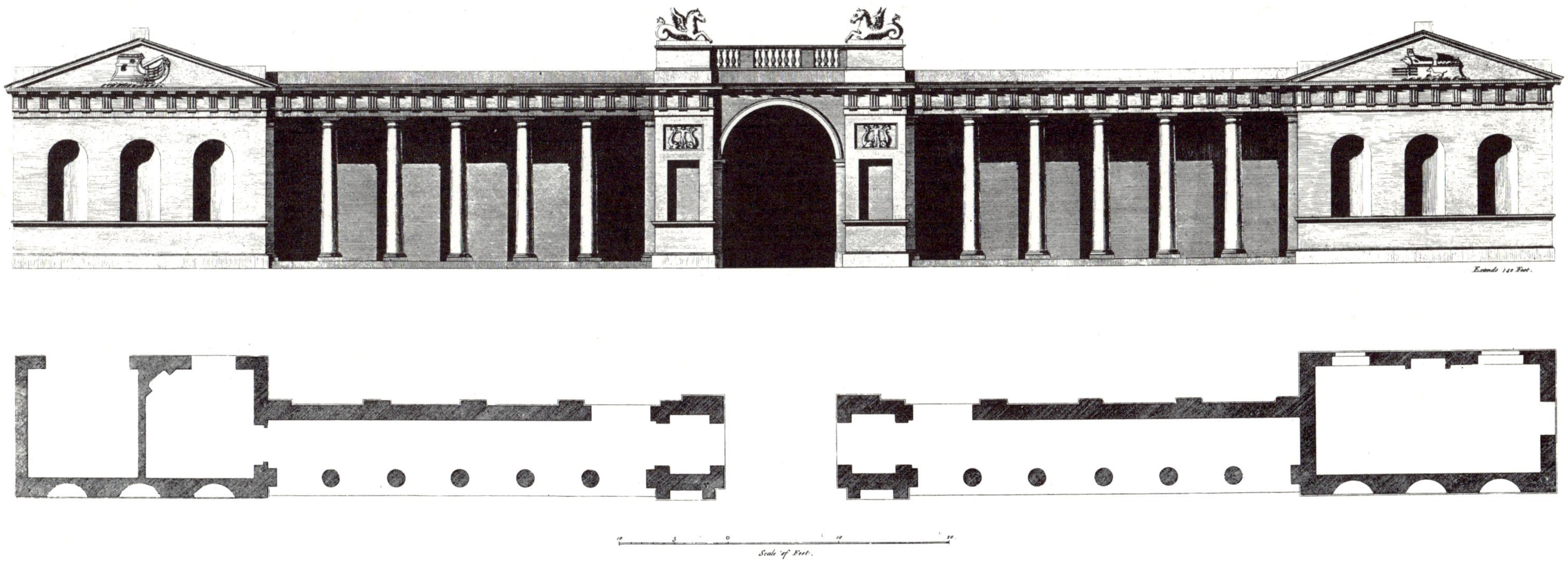

Rob.t Adam Architect Inv.t Delin.t 1760

Publish'd by the Author February the 20th 1761 According to Act of Parliament. And Sold by A. Millar in the Strand. Price 2s. 6d.

F. Patton Sculp.

Vol: I. No. IV. Plate II.

Elevation of a House at Whitehall. Restored as a Board Room for the Paymaster General & Commissioners of Chelsea Hospital, & Office for Invalids.

Elevation du rétablissement d'un ancien Batiment à Whitehall, où s'assemblent le Tresorier et les Commissaires de l'Hôpital de Chelsea, et du Bureau des Invalides.

R. Adam Architect

Published as the Act directs January

R. Blyth sculp.

Design of a Gateway for Carlton House in Pall Mall, for the late Princess Dowager of Wales.

Dessein d'une Porte cochère pour l'Hôtel de Carlton dans Pall Mall, pour la feue Princesse Douairiere de Galles.

Plan of the Gateway

Plan de la Porte Cochère

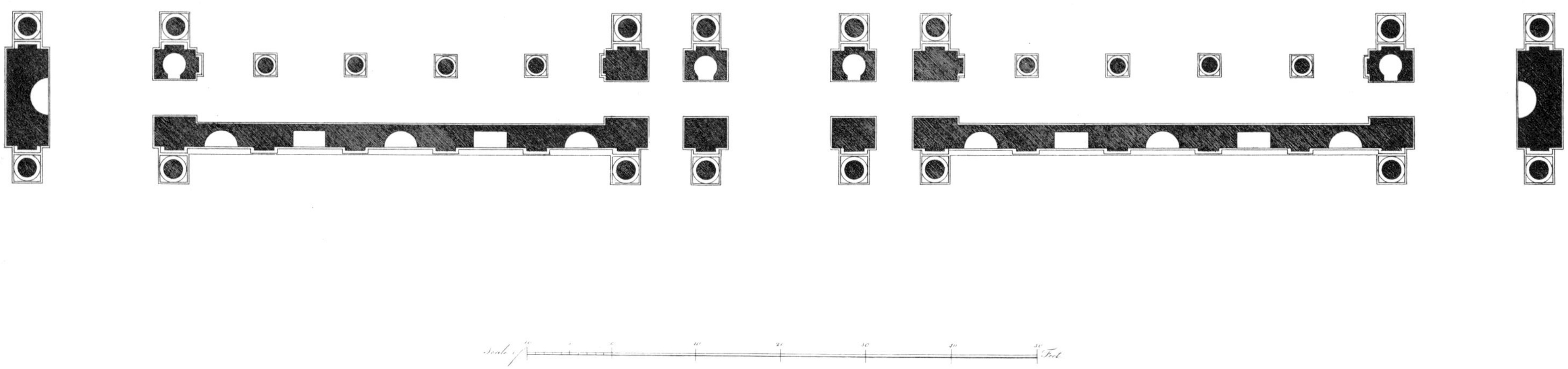

J. Adam Architect 1767

T. Miller Sculp.

Vol. I.
N.º V.
Plate III.
Design of one of the Trophies for the Pediments of the Gateway for Carleton House.
Dessein d'un des Trophées pour les Frontons de la Porte Cochère de la Maison de Carleton.
Design of one of the Trophies over the Columns & Pilasters of the Gateway for Carleton House.
Dessein d'un des Trophées au dessus des Colonnes et Pilastres de la Porte Cochère de la Maison de Carleton.
HONI SOIT QUI MAL Y PENSE
DIEU ET MON DROIT
SPQR
Pannels over the Doors in the Center Building of the Gateway for Carleton House.
Panneaux au dessus des Portes dans le Bâtiment Central de la Porte Cochère de la Maison de Carleton.
Design of the Pateras for the Spandrils of the Arches for the Gateway at Carleton House.
Dessein d'une des Pateras au coté de l'Archivolte des Arcs pour la Porte Cochère de la Maison de Carleton.
J. Adam Architect fig.
Scale of Feet
D. Cunego Sculp. Romæ

No V.

J. Adam Architect 1762

D Cunego sculp Roma

View of the South front of the Deputy-Rangers Lodge in the Green Park.

Vue de la Façade meridionale de la Loge du Deputé Garde-chasse dans le Parc-Vert.

R.t Adam Architect 176[illegible].

Published as the Act directs

T. Vivares sculp.t

Plan of the first floor of the Deputy-Ranger's Lodge in the Green Park.

Plan du prémier Etage de la Loge du Deputé Garde-chasse dans le Parc-Vert.

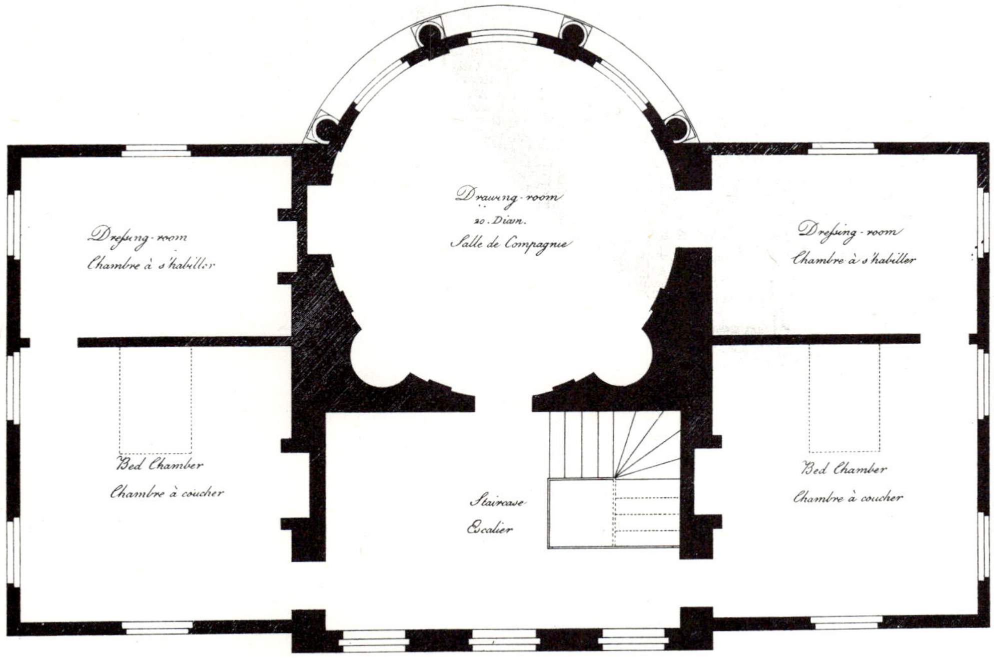

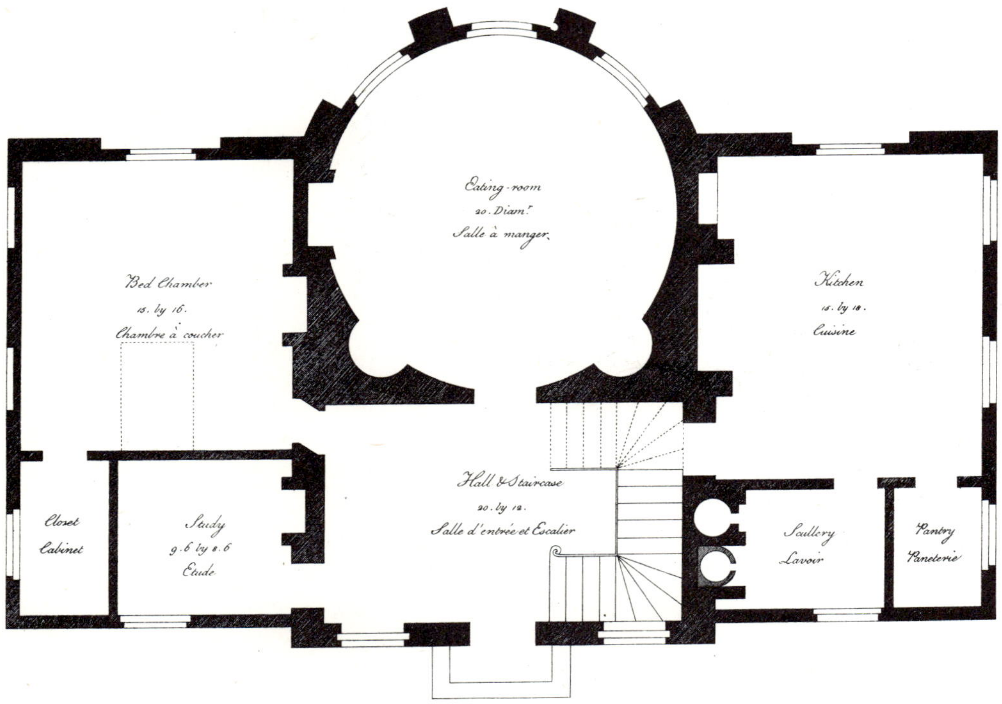

Plan of the Parlor Story of the Lodge
Plan du Rez-de-chaussée de la Loge.

Scale of 10 5 0 10 Feet

Rt. Adam Architect 1768. Published as the Act directs John Roberts incidit

ASHBURNHAM HOUSE

DOVER STREET

LONDON

Adam carried out alterations to Ashburnham House between 1773 and 1776. It is now No. 30 Dover Street.

Plans and elevation of the gateway and porter's lodge. Vol II, No V, Pl V. Engraved by Robert Blyth. *p. 159.*

THE BRITISH COFFEE HOUSE

COCKSPUR STREET

LONDON

Adam remodelled the British Coffee House in 1770. It was demolished in 1886.

Elevation of the principal front and plans of the parlour and principal floors. Vol II, No V, Pl IV. Engraved by Robert Blyth. *p. 160.*

THE THEATRE ROYAL

DRURY LANE

LONDON

In 1775 Adam was commissioned by his friend, David Garrick, to reconstruct and add a new façade to the Theatre Royal, and it seems likely that he had undertaken other alterations to the theatre as early as 1762. The theatre was rebuilt by Henry Holland between 1792 and 1794.

View of the principal front. Vol II, No V, Pl VI. Engraved by P. Begbie. *p. 161.*

View of the interior from the stage. Vol II, No V, Pl VII. Engraved by Benedetto Pastorini. *p. 162.*

BOWOOD PARK

WILTSHIRE

Adam carried out various alterations at Bowood for William Petty, second earl of Shelburne, later the first marquess of Lansdowne, from 1761 to 1771. The estate is currently owned by the present marquess of Lansdowne.

View of the bridge. Vol II, No III, Pl VII. Engraved by Benedetto Pastorini. *p. 163.*

THE PARISH CHURCH

MISTLEY

ESSEX

Adam built Mistley Church between 1776 and 1777. It was demolished in 1870 apart from the twin towers and cupolas, which remain.

View of the south and west fronts. Vol II, No v, Pl III. Engraved by Thomas Vivares. *p. 164.*

Elevation of the south front and plan of the church. Vol II, No v, Pl I. Engraved by John Roberts. *p. 165.*

Elevation of one end and section of the church. Vol II, No v, Pl II. Engraved by John Roberts. *p. 166.*

THE REGISTER HOUSE

PRINCES STREET

EDINBURGH

Robert Adam built the Register House between 1774 and 1792. It exists today as Adam designed it with the exception of the entrance stairs and also of a rear portion completed between 1822 and 1827 by Robert Reid, who made some alterations to the original plans.

Elevation of the principal front. Vol I, No IV, Pl VI. Engraved by John Roberts. *p. 167.*

Plan of the first and second floors. Vol I, No IV, Pl V. No engraver indicated. *p. 168.*

Section of the Register House. Vol I, No IV, Pl VII. Engraved by John Miller. *p. 169.*

THE UNIVERSITY OF EDINBURGH

SOUTHBRIDGE STREET

EDINBURGH

Adam began to plan the University in 1789 but it was not completed until 1834 by W. H. Playfair, and then only to severely modified designs. The dome was built in 1875 by Sir Rowand Anderson.

Elevation of the east front. Vol III, Pl XIV. Engraved by Francis Jukes. *p. 170.*

Elevation of the south front. Vol III, Pl XV. Engraved by Francis Jukes. *p. 171.*

Plan of the principal floor. Vol III, Pl XIII. Engraved by J. W. (?) Harding. *p. 172.*

Elevation of the Gateway & Porters Lodge of Ashburnham House in Dover Street.

Façade de la Porte-cochère et de la Loge du Portier de l'Hôtel d'Ashburnham dans la rüe de Douvre.

Scale of 10 5 0 10 20 Feet

Rt. Adam Architect 1773.

Published as the Act directs 1778.

Rt. Blyth incidit

Vol: II.

Nº V.

Elevation of the British Coffee House.

Façade du Caffé Britannique.

Pl. IIII.

[P]lan of the Parlor Story
Plan du Rez de Chaussée

Plan of the Principal Story
Plan du premier Etage

Scale of 10 5 0 10 20 30 Feet

Rt. Adam Architect 1770.

Published as the Act directs 1778.

Rt. Blyth incidit.

Vol. II. Nº V. Pl. VI.

R. & J. Adam Architects 1775.

View of the New Front towards Bridges Street of the principal Entry to the Theatre Royal Drury Lane.

La Nouvelle Façade vers Bridges Street de la principale Entree du Theatre Royal Drury Lane

R. & J. Adam Architects. Published as the Act directs B. Pastorini Sculp.

Inside View of the Theatre Royal Drury Lane, as it appears from the Stage, altered & decorated in the year 1775.

Vue du Dedans du Théâtre Royal Drury Lane, comme on le voit de la Scène, avec les changemens et décorations faits en 1775.

Design of a Bridge in imitation of the Aqueducts of the Ancients proposed to be built over the Lake at Bowood Park in Wiltshire
One of the Seats of the Earl of Shelburne.

Dessein d'un Pont, en imitation des Aqueducts des Anciens, proposé à être bâti sur le Lac dans le Parc de Bowood dans le Comté de Wilts.
une des Villas du Comte de Shelburne.

R[t]. [Ad]am Architect 1768. Published as the Act directs 1778. Bened: Pastorini, incidit.

South-West View of the Parish Church of Mistley in Essex.

Vüe du Sud-Ouest de l'Eglise Parochiale de Mistley dans le Comté d'Essex.

R^t. Adam Architect 1776

Publish'd as the Act directs 1779

Thos. Vivares sculpt.

South Front of the Parish Church of Mistley in Essex.

Façade Méridionale de l'Eglise Parochiale de Mistley dans le Comté d'Essex.

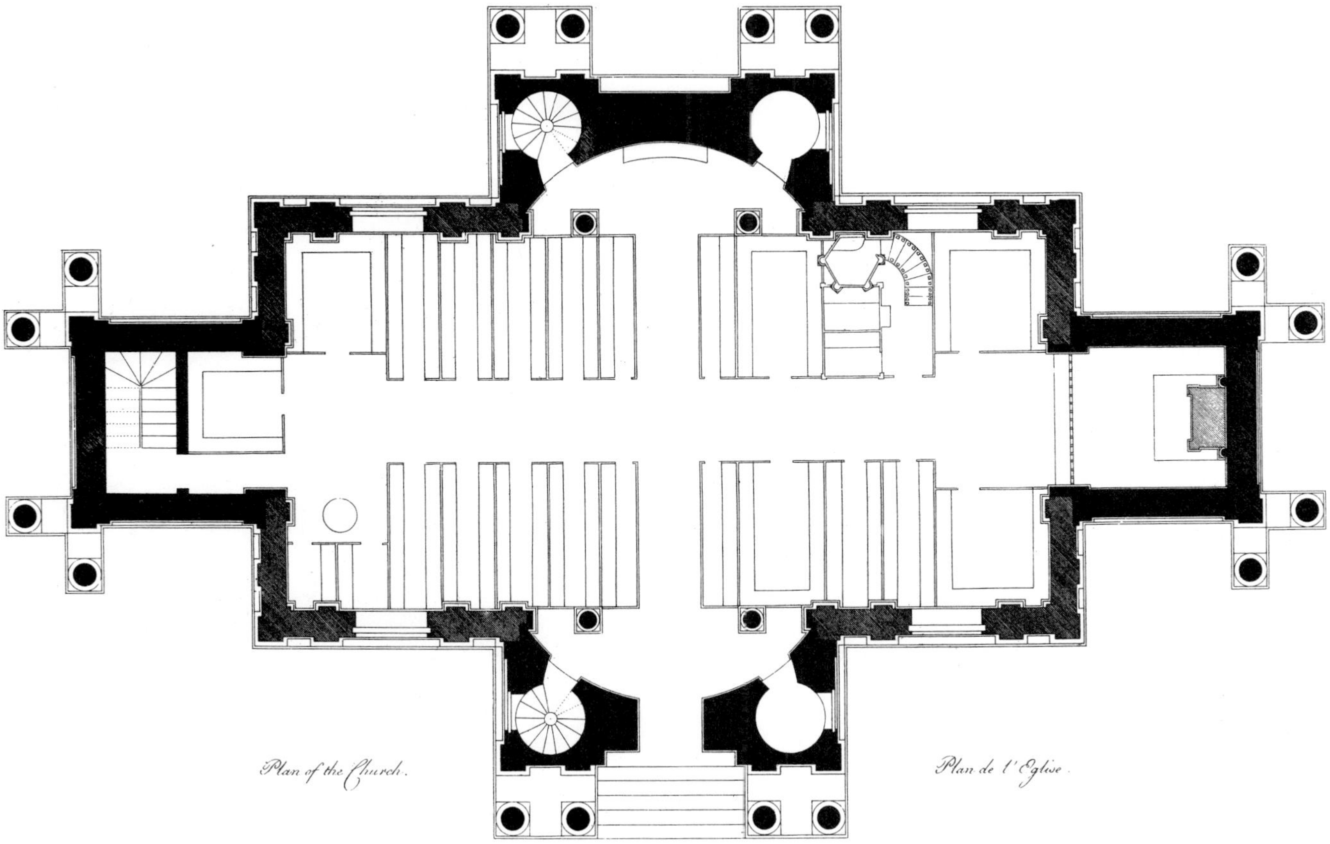

Plan of the Church.

Plan de l'Eglise.

Scale of 10 5 10 20 30 Feet.

R.t Adam Architect 1776.

Published as the Act directs 1779.

John Roberts incidit.

Elevation of one End of the Church at Mistley. Elévation d'un Bout de l'Eglise à Mistley.

Section through the Church, from West to East. Coupe à travers de l'Eglise, de l'Ouest à l'Est.

R. Adam Architect 1776 Published as the Act directs 1779 John Roberts incidit.

South Elevation of the Register Office or Building for containing the Records of Scotland, situated in the New Town of Edinburgh, fronting the Bridge.

Elévation Méridionale du Bureau de Registre ou Batiment pour contenir les Archives de l'Ecosse, situé dans la Nouvelle Ville d'Edinbourg en face du Pont.

Extends 200 Feet.

Scale of 10 5 0 10 20 30 40 50 60 70 80 90 Feet.

R. Adam Architect 1771. Published as the Act directs, January 1773. J. Roberts Sculp.

Plan of the second Story of the Office for the public Records of Scotland.
Plan du second Étage du Bureau pour les Registres publics d'Ecosse.

N.º 1. Room for the Lord Register & Trustees.
2. Passages to the Gallery in the Saloon.
3. Opening of the Saloon in the clear of Gallery.
4. Gallery & Rooms for the General Register.
5. Keeper of the Privy Seal.
6. Offices for Writers to the Privy Seal.
7. Exchequer Records.
8. Heralds Offices.
9. Keeper of the Great Seal.
10. Chancery Records.
11. Office for principal Clerk.
12. D.º for under Clerk.
13. D.º or Rooms for Extractors.
14. Extractors Common Halls.
15. Offices for principal Clerks of Session.
16. D.tto for under Clerks.
17. D.tto for Warrants of Decreets.
18. D.tto for Registration.
19. Exchequer Records.
20. Office for Principal Clerk.
21. D.º for under Clerk.
22. Commissary Records.
23. Office for principal Clerk.
24. D.º for under Clerk.
25. Office for Extractor.
26. Room for Inspection & Extracting of Writs.
27. Waiting Rooms.
28. Staircases.

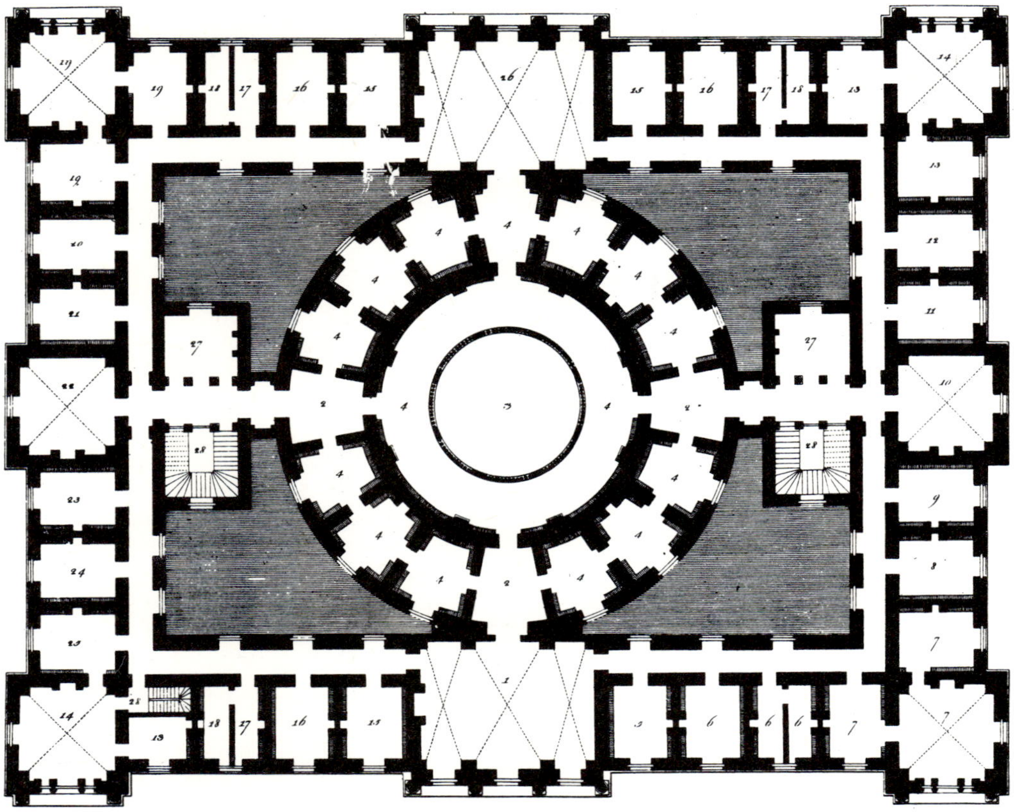

N.º 1. Chambre pour le Seigneur Greffier et les Curateurs.
2. Passages à la Gallerie dans le Salon.
3. Ouverture du Salon dans l'interieur de la Gallerie.
4. Gallerie et Chambres pour le Registre General.
5. Garde du Sceau privé.
6. Bureau pour les Ecrivains du Sceau privé.
7. Registres de l'Echiquier.
8. Bureaux des Hérauts.
9. Garde du Grand Sceau.
10. Registres de la Chancellerie.
11. Bureau du principal Commis.
12. Bureau des sous-Commis.
13. Bureaux ou Chambres des Extracteurs.
14. Salle commune des Extracteurs.
15. Bureaux pour les principaux Commis de Session.
16. Bureaux des sous-Commis de Session.
17. Bureaux d'Expedition de Decrets.
18. Bureaux d'Enregistrement.
19. Registres de l'Echiquier.
20. Bureau du principal Commis.
21. Bureau des sous-Commis.
22. Registres du Commissariat.
23. Bureau du principal Commis.
24. Bureau des sous-Commis.
25. Bureau d'Extracteur.
26. Chambre pour l'Inspection et Extraction des Prises de Corps.
27. Chambres d'attente.
28. Escaliers.

Plan of the first Story of the Office for the public Records of Scotland.
Plan du premier Étage du Bureau pour les Registres publics d'Ecosse.

N.º 1. The Hall.
2. Passages to the Saloon.
3. The Saloon lighted from the Dome in the Center.
4. Offices for Principal Clerks of Session.
5. D.tto for under Clerks.
6. D.tto for Registration.
7. D.tto for Warrants of Registers.
8. D.tto or Closets for Extractors.
9. Extractors Common Halls.
10. Offices for Principal Clerks of Session.
11. D.tto for under Clerks.
12. D.tto for Warrants of Decreets.
13. D.tto or Closets for Extractors.
14. Commissary Records.
15. Sealing Office.
16. Bill Chamber.
17. Teind Office.
18. Writers Hall.
19. Housekeepers Room.
20. Horning Office.
21. Seizines Office.
22. Justiciary Offices.
23. Sheriffs writing Room.
24. Sheriffs Records.
25. Admiralty Offices.
26. Signet Offices.
27. Porters Room.
28. Waiting Rooms.
29. Staircases.
30. Privys.

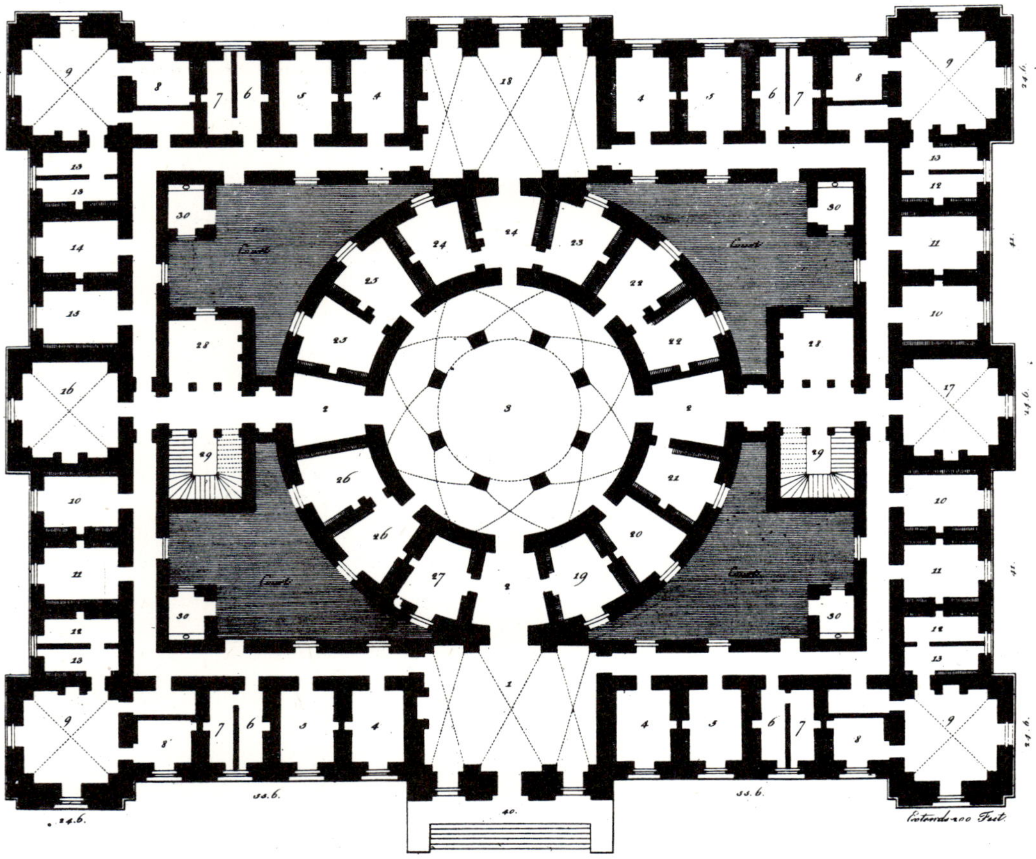

N.º 1. Salle d'Entrée.
2. Passages au Salon.
3. Le Salon, éclairé par le Dome dans le Centre.
4. Bureaux pour les principaux Commis de Session.
5. Bureaux pour les sous-Commis.
6. Bureaux d'Enregistrement.
7. Bureaux pour les Ordres d'Enregistrement.
8. Bureaux ou Cabinets pour les Extracteurs.
9. Salle commune des Extracteurs.
10. Bureaux pour les principaux Commis de Sess.on
11. Bureaux pour les sous-Commis.
12. Bureaux d'Expedition de Décrets.
13. Bureaux ou Cabinets pour les Extracteurs.
14. Registres du Commissariat.
15. Bureau où s'appose le Sceau.
16. Chambre des Bills.
17. Bureau des Dixmes.
18. Salle des Ecrivains.
19. Chambre du Concierge.
20. Bureau pour les Prises de Corps.
21. Bureau des Saisies.
22. Bureaux Justiciers.
23. Chambre à écrire de l'Echevin.
24. Registres de l'Echevin.
25. Bureaux de l'Amirauté.
26. Bureaux du Cachet du Roi.
27. Loge du Portier.
28. Chambres d'attente.
29. Escaliers.
30. Lieux.

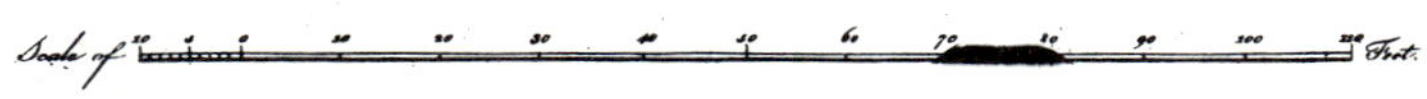

R. Adam Architect 1772.

N.º IV.

Section through the Center Line of the Register Office from North to South.

Coupe par la Ligne Centrale du Bureau de Registre, du Nord au Sud.

Scale of 10 5 0 10 20 30 40 50 60 70 80 90 Feet

R. Adam Architect 1771. | Published as the Act directs January 1772. | T. Miller Sculp.

Design of the East Front of the New Building for the University of Edinburgh

Robert Adam Architect

Publish'd as the Act directs

F. Jukes fecit

Design of the South Front of the New Building for the University of Edinburgh

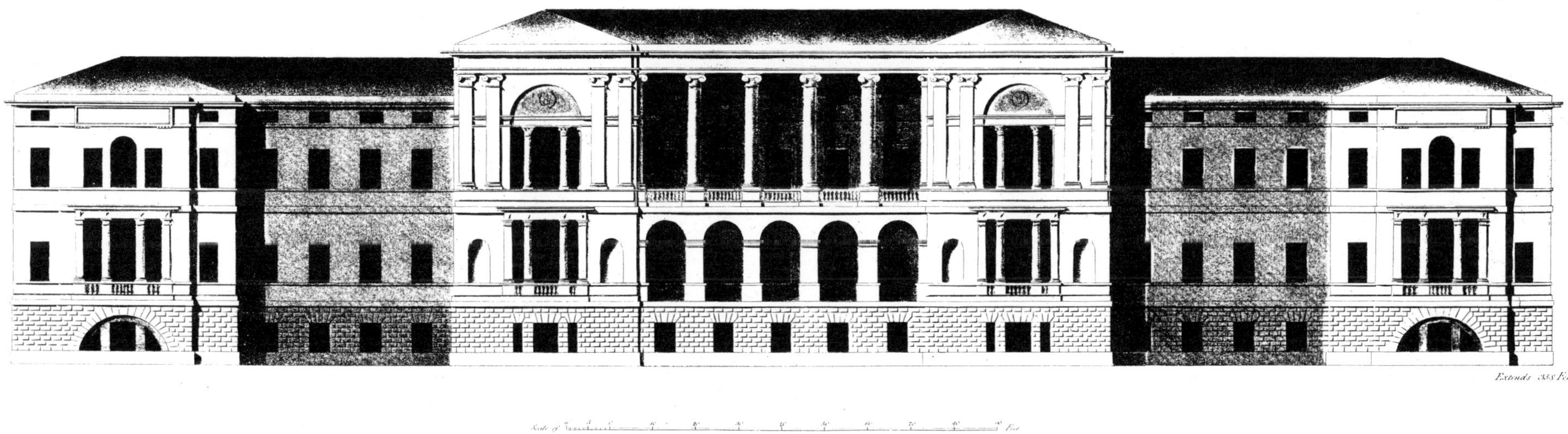

Robert Adam Architect

Published as the Act directs

F. Jukes fecit

Plan of the Principal Story of the New Building for the University of Edinburgh

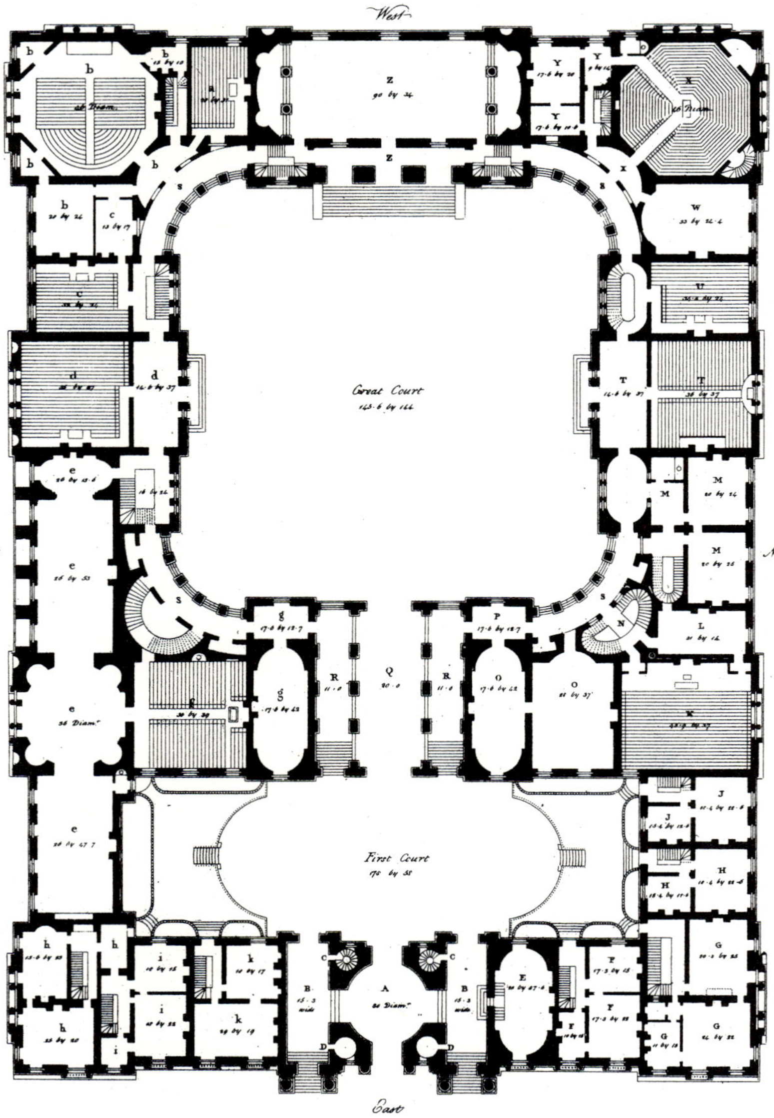

South — North

A *Vestibule or Entrance*
BB *Foot passages*
CC *Stairs to Divinity Class and Janitors houses*
DD *Porters Lodges*
E *Faculty Room or Senatus Academicus*
F *Professors house*
G *Principals house*
H *Professors house*
J *Professors house*
K *Chemistry Class*
L *Preparation room*
M *Professor of Chemistry's house*
N *Stairs to Gallery and upper preparation room of Chemistry Class*
O *Royal Society*
P *Lobby to Royal Society*
Q *Carriage way to Great Court*
RR *Arcades for foot passengers*
SSSS *Corridores of Communication*
T *Lobby and Class for practice of Physick*
U *Civil Law Class*
W *Preparation room or Anatomical Museum*
X *Anatomical Theatre & Lobby*
Y *Painting rooms & private room*
Z *Great Hall for Graduations &c. with Loggia & two stair cases to the Gallerys above.*

a *Class for the Theory of Physick*
b *Mathematical Class Professors room, Instrument room, Lobby &c*
c *Universal History & Antiquity Class, with the Professors room*
d *Class & Lobby for the Professor of Humanity*
e *Museum for Natural History*
f *Class for Natural History*
g *Guard Hall & Lobby*
h *Librarians house*
i *A Professors house*
k *Professor of Divinity's house*

The four houses marked with the Letters F.H.J.& i. to be possessed by the Professors of Humanity, Greek, Hebrew, & Mathematicks. The Senior of these having it in his option to move into the house which may be, vacant, and in case any of these four Professors, should also be Librarian, the Patrons of the University to give the house so rendered vacant, to any other Professor they please during that time

Part of South Bridge Street

Scale of ... *feet*

Robert Adam, Architect. — *Publish'd as the Act directs* — *Harding sculp.*

Nº V.

Design of a painted Ceiling executed in the Room called the Japanned Room, in the Queens House.
Plafond peint executé dans une Chambre nommée la Japonnaise, dans le Palais de la Reine.

Section which shows the coved part of the Ceiling.

Coupe qui fait voir la partie à volute du Plafond.

R. Adam Architect 1762.

Published as the Act directs 1775.

P. Pastorini Sculp.

Design of a Chimney Piece executed in the Great Saloon of the Queens House
Dessein d'une Cheminée executé dans le Grand Salon du Palais de la Reine

A Chimney Piece designed for one of the Rooms in S.t James's Palace
Dessein d'une Cheminée pour une des Chambres dans le Palais de S.t Jacques

R. Adam Architect 1761 — Scale of 12 6 0 1 2 3 Feet — D. Cunego Sculp.

Published as the Act directs 1775

No. V.

Design of a Sedan Chair as executed for Her Majesty.

Dessein d'une Chaise a Porteur executée pour la Reine.

R. Adam Architect 1771

Published as the Act directs 1775

P. Begbie Sculp

Design of the Top of the Harpsicord. Dessein du Dessus du Clavessin.

Elevation of the Harpsicord. Facade du Clavessin.

Plan of the Bottom frame of the Harpsicord. Plan du Bois du Support du Clavessin.

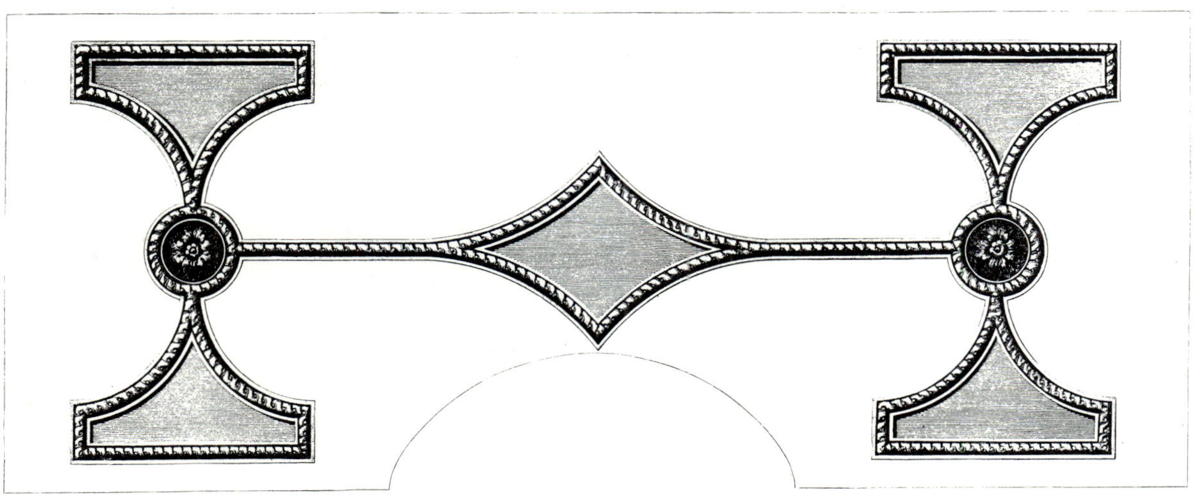

Scale of Feet.

Design of a Harpsicord executed in London, with different Colorred Woods, for The Empress of Russia.

Dessein d'un Clavessin fait a Londres en Bois de Marqueterie, pour L'Impératrice de Russie.

R. Adam Architect. P. Begbie Sculp.

Vol. I.
No 1.
Plate VIII
Design of a Tripod with a Vase and Branches for three Candles.
Dessein d'un tripié et d'un vase portant trois Chandelles.
Design of a Tripod and Vase for Candles.
Dessein d'un tripié et d'un vase servant de Chandelier.
Feet.

Vol: I.
Nº IV
Plate VIII
Lamp for Hanging under Landings of Stairs & between Columns or from the Centers of Arches in Halls, Passages &c.
Lampe pour suspendre au bas d'un Escalier entre des Colomnes aux Centres d'Arches dans des Salles d'entrée, dans des Passages, &c.
Escutchion & Knocker for the outer door of Sir Watkin Williams Wynn Bar.t his House in S.t James's Square, executed in Brass water gilt.
Lamp for Staircases, Halls, Lobbys & passages.
Case for a Watch proposed to be placed upon Tables or Chimney-pieces, & may be executed in Metals, or in Wood gilt.
Etuy pour une Montre, qui on peut mettre sur une Table, ou sur le Chambranle d'une Cheminée, et qui peut être executé en metail, ou en bois doré.
Case for a Watch, to stand on a Table, Commode, or Chimney.
Etuy pour une Montre à mettre sur une Table, une Commode, ou le Chambranle d'une Cheminée.
Watch Case, executed for Lady Apsley's Dressing room.
Etuy à Montre fait pour la Chambre à s'habiller de Milady Apsley.
R. Adam Architect.
Published as the Act directs, January 1775
P. Begbie sculp.

Vol: II.
Nº IV.
Pl: VIII.
Design of a Curtain cornice over a Window.
Dessein d'un rideau de fenêtre.
Design of Furniture for the locks of Doors.
Dessein de Serrures de porte.
Design of a Braket with a Vase for Candles.
Dessein d'un tasseau avec un vase Servant de chandelier.
Design of a vase for Candles, to be fixed to the Wainscoting of a Room.
Dessein d'un vase Servant de lustre
Design of Furniture for the locks of Doors.
Dessein de Serrures de porte.
Handle or nob for Locks of Doors, seen in front.
Poignée de Serrure vue en face.
Handle or Nob of Locks seen on the side.
Poignée de Serrure vue de coté.
Design of Furniture for the locks of Doors.
Dessein de Serrure de porte.
Design of Furniture for the locks of doors.
Dessein de Serrures de porte.
R. Adam Architect 1770
Published as the Act directs 1778
B. Pastorini sculp.

Design of Seat in the Garden of His Grace the Duke of Montagu at Richmond &c.
in which an Antique Pedestal & Vase are proposed to be placed
Dessein d'un petit Pavillon dans le Jardin de Monseigneur le Duc de Montagu à Richmond
dans le quel on proposait de placer un Piédestal et un Vase Antiques.

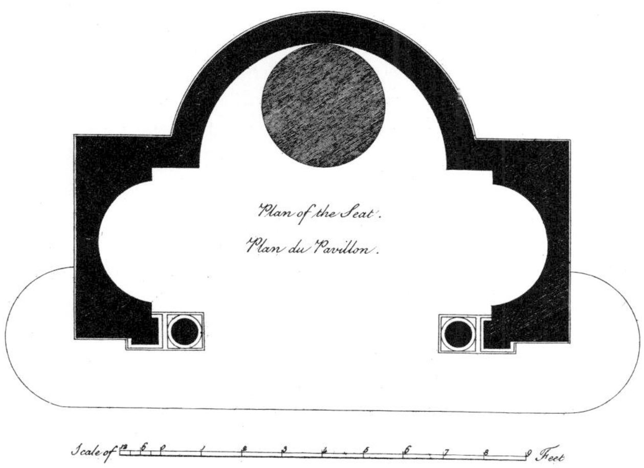

R. Adam Architect 1772. Published as the Act directs 1778. Malpas incidit.

R. Adam Archit. 1762. D. Cunego Sculp. Roma

Original Design of an Illumination & Transparency part of which was executed by Command of the Queen in June 1762 In honour of His Majestys Birthday

Dessein Original d'une Illumination et Transparence dont une partie a été executée par Ordre de la Reine dans le Mois de Juin 1762 en honneur du Jour de la Naissance du Roi

Publish'd as the Act directs 1772.

BIBLIOGRAPHY

The Age of Neo-Classicism (exhibition catalogue for the Council of Europe), London, 1972.

Geoffrey W. Beard, "New Light on Adam's Craftsmen," *Country Life*, cxxxi (10 May 1962).

—, "Robert Adam's Craftsmen," *Connoisseur Year Book*, 1958.

Arthur T. Bolton, *The Architecture of Robert and James Adam, 1758–1794*, London, 1922.

—, "The Classical and Romantic Compositions of Robert Adam," *Architectural Review* (1925).

John Fleming, *Robert Adam and his Circle in Edinburgh and Rome*, London, 1962.

—, "Robert Adam's Castle Style, i and ii," *Country Life* (1968).

Eileen Harris, *The Furniture of Robert Adam*, London, 1963.

—, "Robert Adam and the Gobelins," *Apollo*, lxxvi (April 1962).

John Harris, *Robert Adam and Headfort House*, London, 1973.

Hugh Honour, *Neo-Classicism*, Harmondsworth, 1968.

Christopher Hussey, *English Country Houses, Mid-Georgian, 1760–1800*, London, 1956.

Fiske Kimball, "Les influences anglaises dans la formation du style Louis xvi," *Gazette des Beaux-Arts*, sixth series, v (1931).

—, "The Moor Park Tapestry Suite of Furniture by Robert Adam," *Philadelphia Museum Bulletin*, xxxvi (March 1941).

James Lees-Milne, *The Age of Adam*, London, 1947.

C. Musgrave, *Adam and Heppelwhite and other Neo-Classical Furniture*, London, 1966.

A. P. Oppé, "Robert Adam's Picturesque Compositions," *Burlington Magazine* (1942).

Robert Adam and Scotland (exhibition catalogue for the Scottish Arts Council), Edinburgh, 1972.

Fritz Saxl and Rudolf Wittkower, *British Art and the Mediterranean*, Oxford, 1948.

John Steegman and C. K. Adam, "The Iconography of Robert Adam," *Architectural Review* (1942).

Damie Stillman, *The Decorative Work of Robert Adam*, London, 1966.

—, "Robert Adam and Piranesi," *Essays in the History of Architecture presented to Rudolf Wittkower*, London, 1967.

Sir John Summerson, *Architecture in Britain, 1530–1830*, Harmondsworth, 1953.

—, *Georgian London*, London, 1945.

John Swarbrick, *Robert Adam and his Brothers*, London, 1915.

R. W. Symond, "Adam and Chippendale: a Myth Exploded," *Country Life Annual*, 1958.

Maurice Tomlin, "Back to Adam at Osterley," *Country Life*, cxlvii (18 and 25 June 1970).

—, *Catalogue of Adam Period Furniture* (Victoria and Albert Museum), London, 1972.

Margaret Whinney, *Home House, No. 20 Portman Square*, London, 1969.

Doreen Yarwood, *Robert Adam*, London, 1970.

A. J. Youngson, *The Making of Classical Edinburgh*, Edinburgh, 1966.

INDEX OF BUILDINGS

The numbers in *italics* refer to pages on which illustrations will be found.

INDEX OF ENGRAVERS

In addition, several of the engravings were published without signatures. These anonymous engravings have not been included in this index.